DRUG

CORRUPTION, COUNTERINSURGENCY AND COVERT OPERATIONS IN THE THIRD WORLD

WARS

JONATHAN MARSHALL

COHAN & COHEN PUBLISHERS

Cohan & Cohen Publishers
Post Office Box 1099
Forestville, California 95436

First Printing

Cover design: Visual Strategies, San Francisco
Typesetting: Pteragraphics

Library of Congress Cataloging-in-Publication Data

Marshall, Jonathan.
    Drug wars: corruption, counterinsurgency, and covert operations in the Third World/by Jonathan Marshall.
    ii, 90p., 7 p. plates ; 21.5 cm
    Includes bibliographical references and index.
    ISBN 1-56060-062-4: $14.95
    1. Narcotics, Control of—United States. 2. Narcotics, Control of—Developing countries. 3. Corruption (in politics)—United States. 4. Corruption (in politics)—Developing countries. 5. United States—Foreign relations—1945- 5. Counterinsurgency—Developing countries. I. Title.
HV5825.M355 1990   90-49574
363.4'5'091724—dc20   CIP

TABLE OF CONTENTS

Preface

Millions of Americans who smoke marijuana, snort cocaine or shoot up heroin take for granted the long supply lines that deliver the mood-altering chemicals they demand. From foreign fields, across seas and through borders, the drugs reach America's streets despite the Herculean efforts of police, prosecutors and judges. As the media remind Americans almost daily, the country is awash in illegal drugs of every kind.

Politicians and police, frustrated by the impossibility of patrolling every alley and arresting every pusher, blame the countries of origin for America's drug epidemic. In a major report to the nation in 1989, drug czar William Bennett declared that "we must...disrupt the transportation and trafficking of drugs within their source countries, since the interdiction of drugs and traffickers en route to the United States is an immensely more complicated, expensive, and less effective means of reducing the drug supply to this country." Or as Sen. William Cohen of Maine remarked in 1989, "Shouldn't we be looking at ways in which to invoke the military...to go to the source or go to where the machine gun nests are as opposed to trying to catch the bullets that are being fired into the United States?"[1]

Like Cohen, other federal officials routinely adopt military metaphors to describe their efforts to suppress illicit narcotics. Since President Reagan signed a directive in 1986 defining drugs as a threat to "national security," Washington policy makers have exploited the image of war to quiet public dissent and mobilize support for dizzy increases in drug enforcement spending.

In the Third World, thanks in part to U.S. political pressure and military aid, the "war on drugs" is not merely an overworked metaphor. It is fast becoming a bloody reality. Green Beret trainers are at work in Colombia, Peru, Ecuador and Bolivia and much of Central America. Congress has appropriated unprecedented levels of military aid to

Colombia, Peru, and Bolivia, mostly for fighting the drug traffic: $118 million in fiscal 1991, on top of a nearly equal amount in 1990. As we shall see, such aid often goes to forces that either serve the drug lords or control the traffic themselves. And sometimes, we shall further see, American leaders accept that outcome as the price of achieving other aims sold to the nation under the false banner of drug enforcement.

Just as war is the continuation of politics by other means, so the "war on drugs" has become an extension of foreign policy by other means. The ideology and practice of drug enforcement have served too often to advance the goals of counterinsurgency, cold war propaganda and U.S. covert operations in the Third World. These goals do not fairly characterize all U.S. narcotics programs overseas nor the motives of many individual government officials or drug agents. But the frequent distortions of drug policy documented here illustrate the dangerous potential for cynical leaders to misdirect programs whose overwhelming popularity discourages critical oversight.

This brief study does not focus on the political economy or culture of drugs in the Third World, topics already scrutinized by numerous other writers and scholars. Nor does it pretend to offer an insider's account of the bureaucratic politics of drug policy making in the U.S. government. Instead, it explores the ways in which drug enforcement has been systematically subordinated to larger foreign policy objectives. The American people, and Congress, cannot meaningfully debate national drug policy in the face of ignorance or silence about those true objectives.

Many people contributed valuable information or insights to this study. I would like to thank in particular Jack Blum, Bob Callahan, John Hill, John Kelly, Ted Rubinstein, Peter Dale Scott, Bill Walker, Dave White, Coletta Youngers, and the Data Center in Oakland. I would also like to thank the Pacific Research Institute for Public Policy in San Francisco, for permission to reprint and rework portions of my essay "Drugs and U.S. Foreign Policy," in Ronald Hamowy, ed., *Dealing with Drugs: Consequences of Government Control* (San Francisco, 1987). And I thank my family for their love, support, and patience.

Oakland, California

Chapter I

Going to the Source

The idea of coöperating with foreign governments when we know their elements are corrupt is both dangerous and stupid. The people we're supposed to be helping are shooting at us.
—Jack Blum, former congressional drug investigator[2]

It is impossible to break up the traffic in drugs because of the corruption of the police and special agents and also because of the wealth and political influence of some of the traffickers.
—Leopoldo Salazar, head of Mexican Federal Narcotics Service, 1931[3]

International narcotics control rests upon the central premise—or pretense—that by helping foreign governments stamp out drugs abroad, the United States can avoid curbing its own demand for them at home.

The reality is all too different. Time after time, the very governments and foreign security agencies Washington supports with anti-drug assistance shield the drug kings or monopolize the traffic themselves. Corruption knows no borders. Exposure of the "French Connection" showed that drug profits ensnare politicians, police and intelligence officials even in a First World nation like France, with its strong tradition of professionalism.[4] Plenty of drug corruption scandals in the United States itself prove the same point.

Such corruption often follows a progression as it becomes entrenched. Drug enforcement is a form of market regulation and Darwinian selection. Police weed out traffickers less skilled at evading detection or buying protection. "Efficient" traffickers develop a symbiotic relationship with ambitious agents of the law. Police need underworld informants to make their cases; successful traffickers in turn need police to block their rivals. Both have an incentive to arrest large numbers of weak, unprotected competitors. These mutual needs may, and often do, promote outright coöperation and corruption.

Over time police may come to realize that taking bribes offers fewer rewards than dealing the drugs themselves, while still using drug laws to eliminate independent competitors. In extreme cases, drug profits may even strengthen corrupt police or military elites vis-a-vis other government institutions to the point where they seize state power, as the Bolivian military did in the infamous 1980 "cocaine coup."

In the Third World particularly, where government institutions have short histories and questionable legitimacy, officials may rationalize their takeover of lucrative drug rackets as needed to preëmpt independent syndicates that threaten state power. Failure to bring those independent traffickers under control can lead to internal chaos, civil war or warlordism. As the United Nations International Narcotics Control Board noted in its 1984 annual report, "Illegal drug production and trafficking financed by organized crime is so pervasive that the economies of entire countries are disrupted, legal institutions menaced and the very security of some states threatened."[5] Once again, the problem is not unique to the Third World. Even Italy had to send an anti-terrorist commander (Gen. Carlo Alberto Dalla Chiesa) to combat Mafia strongholds in Sicily—and he was brazenly assassinated.

Where efforts to suppress drugs produce instability, not security, authorities may try to take control of the drug traffic rather than wage continual war against it. Using drug laws and armed force as weapons against independent competitors, governments can create *de facto* drug monopolies to help consolidate their power within the national territory. Chiang Kai-shek used that classic tactic in his campaign to unify China under his party, the Kuomintang (KMT). By seizing poppy fields and monopolizing drug marketing channels in the name of opium "suppression," he undercut independent warlords financed from regional drug profits. Ironically, in the 1940s the U.S. Federal Bureau of Narcotics trained Chiang's secret police—who ganged up with the head of the Shanghai underworld to run what may have been the world's largest drug trafficking syndicate.[6]

Similar symptoms of gross corruption afflict country after country where drugs are produced or transshipped:

BOLIVIA

Staggering under the burden of widespread unemployment, foreign debt and the loss of tin as a major foreign exchange earner, Bolivia survives only by the grace of cocaine. Coca leaf and cocaine production account for roughly 30 percent of gross domestic product, employ some 20 percent of the working population and dwarf all other export products in value. Three quarters of a million people depend on coca directly for their livelihood. Few Bolivian leaders, understandably, favor committing national suicide by really stamping out their country's only significant source of wealth.[7]

The U.S. General Accounting Office (GAO) reported in 1988 that Bolivia's illicit drug trade had grown at an annual rate of 35 percent a year since 1980, owing in part to "an unprecedented level corruption which extends to virtually every level of Bolivian government and Bolivian society," including the "police, military and judicial systems." A State Department assessment concluded in early 1990 that Bolivia's performance "in almost every area indicates total lack of commitment to the drug war."[8]

Even before the drug boom of the 1980s, however, the coca market enjoyed powerful political protection. Official complicity in the traffic marked the reign of Gen. Hugo Banzer from 1971 to 1978. Banzer seized power with financing from a syndicate of coca wholesalers; one of his ranches housed a plant for processing coca paste into cocaine. During his rule, state banks financed the boom in Bolivia's cocaine industry. Ironically, in 1976 Secretary of State Henry Kissinger offered Banzer millions of dollars to train Bolivia's narcotics police and fund coca eradication programs.[9]

Bolivia suffered another, and much more notorious, "cocaine coup" in 1980 after top officers sat down with six of the country's leading traffickers to negotiate protection payments. Gen. Luis Garcia Meza came away $1 million richer. He and a band of military drug profiteers subcontracted security services for the drug lords to a group of notorious international fascists led by fugitive Nazi war criminal Klaus Barbie. The Carter administration withdrew its ambassador to protest the regime's human rights abuses and drug record.[10]

Bolivia's liberation from the grip of brutal cocaine officers a couple of years later did not free its economy from dependence on drugs. Even honest officials have not dared take on the militant and well-organized peasant syndicates that protect coca cultivators. For all the government's show of drug enforcement, a U.S. congressional study concluded in 1985 that "not one hectare of coca leaf has been eradicated since the United States established the narcotics assistance program in 1971."[11]

U.S. DEA agents and Special Forces troops have worked diligently to build Bolivia's anti-drug police, known as the "Leopards." But the Leopards have proven more efficient at collecting bribes than curbing cocaine. The unit's first commander took "gratuities" from the traffickers, delayed raids on their behalf and finally tried to overthrow the government in June 1984. Ed Merwin, the chief U.S. narcotics police adviser from 1984 to 1986, oversaw eight different commanders, "mostly because they either got too blatant about accepting bribes or, in the one case of the only really good tactical field commander we had, he refused to take a bribe and he got fired by his boss, who had offered him the bribe." Merwin concluded that "a hundred percent of the Bolivian enforcement structure was corrupted." As of 1989, DEA officers estimated that about half of Leopard commanders took payoffs from the traffickers.[12]

The corruption doesn't stop there. In October 1988, the head of the army's largest regiment and four of his top officers were cashiered for protecting a drug airstrip. Around the same time, Washington suspended assistance to Bolivia's navy—which patrols the landlocked nation's rivers—after navy officers held two DEA agents incommunicado at gunpoint and helped several traffickers escape arrest by the Leopards. Interior Minister Fernando Barthelemy, who oversaw all anti-drug operations, resigned in February 1987 after a committee of Bolivia's congress accused him of taking bribes to hold up a raid on one of the country's biggest drug labs.[13]

Bolivian leaders know the score as well as anyone. That's why Daniel Cabezas, chairman of the Bolivian Senate's Commission on Drug Trafficking, came out in December 1989 against turning his country's military loose on the traffickers. "There is a serious risk that the armed forces could be corrupted by the cancer of drug trafficking," he observed. "...This is too dangerous for such an important institution as the military, which has the responsibility of protecting us."[14]

COLOMBIA

The home of the Medellin and Cali "cartels" earns roughly as much money exporting cocaine to the rest of the world as it does from coffee, a legal and milder stimulant. The president of Colombia's banking association estimated in 1988 that cocaine accounted for about one-ninth of the country's gross domestic product, a huge fraction considering the country's relatively advanced economy.[15] Colombia also remains a major producer of marijuana, behind only the United States and Mexico.

Drug profits have corrupted every corner of Colombian society, starting with its law enforcement agencies. The Departamento Administrativo Seguridad (DAS), roughly equivalent to the FBI, was particularly notorious under the leadership of Gen. Jorge Ordonez Valderrama in the 1970s. His ruthless subordinates robbed independent cocaine dealers, then resold their stashes. Three provincial DAS chiefs were arrested on drug charges before Ordonez himself was finally jailed for embezzlement.[16]

Other units also had their hands in the trade. Greedy Customs agents even did battle with DAS forces for control of a major drug shipment. And in 1976 the entire top command of the national police narcotics unit was implicated in drug crimes by a former agent.[17]

At Washington's instigation, Colombia sent its military to combat drug traffickers in the remote Guajira Peninsula in late 1978. But smugglers had corrupted the defense ministry, which prevented honest police actions against known traffickers. Noted one U.S. congressional delegation, "The Guajira campaign appears to have been a great deterrent to the small unorganized trafficker; however, there is still a significant amount of marijuana available for the major trafficking networks."[18]

Worse than that, in 1983 an officer who would rise to head Colombia's Ministry of Defense commanded special troops who transported an entire cocaine laboratory to the Brazilian border under the pretense of fighting guerrillas.[19]

The murder of the country's attorney general by narcotraffickers in May 1984 aroused a national furor. Political leaders vowed to punish the drug mafia. Many bosses were indeed driven underground, but authorities seized few drug caches. One cynical newspaper discovered a new disease, "mafia blindness," that had infected police investigating teams.[20]

After a brief sojourn in Panama, the drug lords returned to business as usual in Colombia. As before, they relied on friendly military and police units to eliminate small-time competitors. Offers of silver or lead—bribes or bullets—kept the judiciary in line. In January 1988, Colombia's attorney general took a lethal dose of lead from drug-financed assassins. He had been investigating the Minister of Justice and two judges, among other officials, for involvement in the release from jail of Medellin cocaine kingpin Jorge Ochoa.[21]

Corruption within the elite DAS continues to keep many high-level targets one step ahead of police raids. In mid-1989, Bogota television reported that the traffickers appeared to "have access to practically all confidential government information, such as minutes of cabinet meetings" and those of the National Drug Council and Supreme Court of Justice. The narcos apparently even succeeded in penetrating the U.S. embassy to read some of its cable traffic.[22]

By late 1989, the attorney general's office had no fewer than 4,200 corruption cases under investigation involving the national police and 1,700 involving the armed forces.[23]

MEXICO

In recent years, Mexico has been the largest single source country for heroin and marijuana entering the United States and the transit country for one-third or more of all the cocaine moving north across the border. In late 1984, police discovered one 10,000-ton marijuana farm, enough to satisfy the entire U.S. market for a year and eight times as much as previous estimates of Mexico's entire annual production.[24]

Corruption—which Alan Riding has called "both the glue that holds the Mexican system together and the oil that makes it work"—helps account for the longterm invulnerability of so many major traffickers. The problem goes all the way to the top. The wife of Mexican President Luis Echeverria reportedly had ties to the notorious Mexican-based smuggler Alberto Sicilia-Falcon in the early 1970s. Echeverria's successor, Jose Lopez Portillo, reportedly amassed a multi-million dollar fortune from payoffs.[25]

President Miguel de la Madrid got off to a good start in late 1982 by firing Mexico City's chief of police, whose vast fortune did not accord with his humble salary. U.S. and Mexican intelligence files reportedly named him as a protector of the illegal heroin trade, as well as a brutal murderer of rival traffickers.[26]

But de la Madrid may simply have been ridding himself of a rival rather than cleaning house. "Mexico hasn't arrested a major drug trafficker in eight years," DEA Administrator Francis Mullen, Jr. charged in early 1985 after authorities failed to make any progress in solving the kidnap-murder of U.S. drug agent Enrique Camarena. "They let the suspects get away. Then they start the raids."[27]

Under immense pressure that year, the government of de la Madrid fired hundreds of agents from the Federal Judicial Police and Directorate of Federal Security (DFS), admitting to "criminal links between narcotics traffickers and police agents." Members of both organizations had acted as bodyguards for some of Mexico's top drug criminals and supplied them with official credentials. The DFS not only established giant plantations capable of growing thousands of tons of marijuana, but even organized the notorious Guadalajara Cartel, responsible for shipping tons of cocaine every month into the United States. Meanwhile, entire state police organizations handled security for the leading drug syndicates. And the military supplied caravans to move shipments to the U.S. border.[28]

Despite the purge, drug supplies rose and seizures fell. Between 1986 and 1987, marijuana production jumped 50 percent and heroin output shot up 70 percent. The U.S. Customs Service went on record in 1988, singling out "endemic" corruption as the "most important fact which undermines effective and meaningful narcotics cooperation with Mexico."[29]

Since President Carlos Salinas de Gortari took charge following a disputed election in 1988, the situation has improved. Government forces have rounded up such powerful and once-untouchable traffickers as Miguel Felix Gallardo. They arrested the last chief of DFS for the murder of a muckraking newspaper columnist who threatened to expose his links to the drug trade. Police also arrested the former head of Interpol in Mexico, who used to oversee the country's drug investigations.[30]

But some notorious traffickers and their agents continue to receive favored treatment despite these purges. The Mexican armed forces, particularly in the northern zone, show disturbing signs of drug corruption. And the Mexican press has raised questions about several key members of the Salinas government, from the attorney general down to Mexico City's police chief, a former head of the infamous DFS.[31]

A U.S. intelligence assessment from 1979 still holds: Corruption so permeates the government that "any wholesale housecleaning would cause cracks in the power structure."[32]

PERU

Responsible for producing more than half the cocaine shipped to the United States, Peru depends on more than 200,000 acres of coca for as much as a quarter of its gross domestic product.[33] With hyperinflation raging in the four-digit range, foreign exchange reserves depleted, the economy shrinking and a fanatical left-wing insurgency terrorizing much of the country, coca production may be one of the few "bright" spots on the Peruvian scene.

Or at least that's how it may seem to the tens of thousands of peasants who make their living growing and harvesting the traditional Andean coca leaf for export—and to the countless underpaid government officials who look the other way in return for bribes.

Peru ranks with Bolivia for the sheer ubiquity of corruption throughout government ranks.

The military has had its hand in the cocaine trade ever since 1949, when the government established a state coca monopoly and set aside all profits for the construction of military barracks.[34] In the brief period from July 1984 to December 1985, when the army exercised emergency powers over the center of Peruvian coca cultivation, the Upper Huallaga Valley, drug production soared. The army confined the anti-drug police to their barracks while chasing leftwing Sendero Luminoso (Shining Path) guerrillas. Army officers reportedly raked in hundreds of thousands of dollars for protecting the drug lords during those operations. "It's better for the narcos when the army is here," said one police official.[35] The government finally had to pull the army out before it became a total appendage of the drug elite.[36] When the army returned to the Upper Huallaga Valley in 1989, however, it once again declared major drug regions "off-limits" to Peruvian police and DEA agents. Soldiers loading cocaine paste onto transport planes have reportedly even fired on U.S.-piloted anti-drug helicopters.[37]

In 1982, a former Peruvian air force general was sentenced to 15 years in prison after being caught with 5 kilos of cocaine on his way to Miami.[38] The same year the war minister accused two former ministers of interior with conspiring to undertake a major cocaine deal.[39]

In 1985, a huge drug scandal prompted President Alan Garcia to dismiss at least 100 air force personnel, more than 200 top officers from Peru's three national police forces and well over 1,000 policemen. Several hundred judges also came under investigation for suspected corruption.[40]

Yet corruption remains endemic to Peruvian law enforcement. In 1988, the State Department's top narcotics official admitted that allegations of corruption were still "swirling around the PIP," Peru's FBI.[41] A congressional staff report confirmed that "repeated compromises of DEA information [through PIP] eventually led to a virtual termination of relationship between the two agencies" and added that "corruption in all segments of the Peruvian government continues to impede meaningful antinarcotics efforts."[42]

The politicians are no cleaner. In late 1988, West German police arrested a leader of Peru's ruling party, APRA, while attempting to cash a large check signed by one of Peru's most notorious traffickers.[43] Around the same time, the head of President Alan Garcia's press office was arrested with two satchels of cocaine; he used his influence to destroy the police file but was later unmasked.[44] Suspicions of APRA's deep involvement in the drug trade fed reports that the Garcia government purposedly ignored widespread coca trafficking in the Cuzco area in the southern part of the country.[45]

THAILAND

Though not itself a major heroin producer, Thailand is the primary outlet for heroin produced by border laboratories inside Burma. Ethnic Chinese syndicates in Bangkok and the northern city of Chiang Mai handle the drugs for export. Thai law enforcement officers have never seriously cracked down on them, perhaps because as much as half the economy's international financial transfers relate to drugs.[46]

In 1977, Rep. Lester Wolff, head of the House narcotics committee, reported that one of Bangkok's top drug wholesalers had "a knack for making friends in Thai government circles. He has close connections with the Thai army and the Thai police as well as officials of the former government."[47] A contemporary news account declared that "The entire middle level of the Thai official and police establishment is riddled with corruption and graft."[48]

Corruption and politics have also kept the government from touching drug traffickers in the remote hill country of the opium-rich "Golden Triangle." There, remnants of the Nationalist KMT armies forced out of China in 1949 settled and made a livelihood out of smuggling. In return for Bangkok's sanction they provided intelligence and even counterinsurgency assistance against leftist revolutionaries in the region. Indeed, according to one DEA report, the opium-smuggling former KMT General Li Wen-huan used Thai air force helicopters sent from Chiang Mai for his operations.[49]

As a result, noted one congressional report in 1977, "Thai police are permitted to mount operations against minor smugglers [but] not allowed to interfere at the higher levels of opium politics which provide the armies with their financial support. The result is a charade for international consumption in which roughly 3 percent of the narcotics are seized and several score of traffickers arrested yearly, while the principal organizations of the trade continue unimpeded."[50]

Nothing much has changed since then. Among the leading officials implicated in narcotics trafficking in recent years have been the commander of the Chiang Mai provincial police, a major general in the national police, and at least two former prime ministers.[51] According to one respected Bangkok newspaper, "Widespread corruption allows more than 90 percent of [Golden] Triangle drugs to filter through the country."[52] And although DEA spokesmen from time to time tout Thailand as "a consistent ally in drug control objectives," the GAO has cited "endemic corruption that exists among officials charged with narcotics control responsibilities."[53]

Such overwhelming evidence of pervasive and ineradicable corruption in the major producing or trafficking countries inevitably raises the question: Are U.S. policy makers merely quixotic in pursuing the hopeless quest for a solution at the source? Or do they value foreign narcotics programs, despite their failure to stop drugs, as a means of advancing less obvious policy goals?

Chapter II

Drug Enforcement as Counterinsurgency

While the ultimate purpose of the military assistance, including equipment and training...is to combat narcotics trafficking and production, it is inevitable that counter-narcotics activities will at times require counter-insurgency efforts to regain government control over certain areas.
—Letter from Department of State congressional liaison Janet Mullins to Rep. Dante Fascell, D-Fl., April 1990.[54]

Fully aware that corruption undermines American efforts to root out drugs at their source, Congress requires the executive branch to "certify" that foreign aid recipients are acting in good faith against the traffickers. The certification process is an open invitation to bad faith by the administration, however. State Department officials intent on maintaining good foreign relations and DEA chiefs interested in keeping a presence abroad whitewash corruption that makes a mockery of their efforts. As one DEA agent in Mexico complained a few years ago, "We're perpetuating a fraud just by being there."[55]

Mathea Falco, former head of the State Department's narcotics office, should know. "The whole certification process is a joke," she observed. "Countries that everybody knows are not coöperating with us, we have to say are coöperating because of political interests... So we end up decertifying countries like Iran. We might has well decertify Mars. This has absolutely no relation to a rational foreign policy."[56]

This irrationality arises inevitably from the conflict between opportunistic drug-war rhetoric and the reality that other interests often take precedence over narcotics enforcement. Chief among those has long been the containment of Communism. As one DEA official remarked when challenged about the Jamaican government's blatant toleration of the marijuana trade, "The issue is should we press them to do things which could result in the election and installation of a leftist government, as they've had in the previous administration. Drugs are a serious problem. But Communism is a greater problem."[57]

Such priorities suggest that blindness and inadvertence may not be all that lead the United States, in the name of fighting drugs, to assist the very military and police forces most implicated in the traffic. To be sure, a great many different bureaucratic and policy interests shape U.S. drug programs—more often in conflict and confusion than in smooth concert. It would be a mistake to read clear intentions into the unintended consequences of those programs.

Too often, however, decision makers have demonstrably twisted U.S. drug enforcement programs to bolster "friendly" but repressive governments abroad. They have exploited public passions and the widespread sense of urgency over drug abuse to bypass congressional restrictions on foreign police assistance and, in collusion with local security forces, to suppress political dissent and armed insurgencies. These programs will continue, even with the demise of the Cold War, so long as Washington resorts to violent means of countering political threats to its interests in the Third World.

Occasional admissions of this hidden agenda have surfaced in the public record. Richard Brown, the top Pentagon policy maker for Latin America, explained the Bush administration's emphasis on military aid to fight drugs: "In Peru and Colombia, you have counterinsurgency going on as well, and in many cases, they are very closely linked, and that's what we're trying to reinforce as well."[58] Robert Gelbard, Brown's counterpart in the State Department, observed in 1988 that "because of the completely close links interwining the terrorist guerrilla movements and the drug traffickers there is a clear necessity for the armed forces of those countries...to have significantly greater military resources to combat the insurgent movements."[59]

Gelbard's assertion that guerrillas and traffickers enjoy "completely close links" is highly controversial to say the least. As a general rule, the two groups have widely divergent agendas: Guerrillas want to overthrow the system while traffickers want to profit from it. The former aim to destroy the bourgeoisie; the latter seek to join it. A totalitarian movement like Shining Path in Peru, which taxes the drug trade to finance its operations, would probably slit the throat of every trafficker upon taking power. But the "narco-guerrilla" image popularized in the Reagan years provides an ideal cover for pushing a counterinsurgency agenda in the guise of narcotics enforcement.[60]

One particularly candid military officer, Col. John Waghelstein of the Special Forces, made this ploy explicit in a 1987 article in *Military Review*. Decrying the public's post-Vietnam reluctance to support Third World interventions, he argued that a "melding in the public mind" of the alleged links between drug traffickers and insurgents would make it difficult for Congress to "stand in the way of supporting our allies with the training, advice, and security assistance" necessary to fight Marxist guerrillas:

> Those church and academic groups that have slavishly supported insurgency in Latin America would find themselves on the wrong side of the moral issue... Instead of responding defensively to each insurgency on a case-by-case basis, we could act in concert with our allies. Instead of wading through the legislative snarl and financial constraints that characterize our security assistance posture, we could act with alacrity to the threat. Instead of debating each separate threat, we can begin to see the hemisphere as a whole and ultimately develop the vision that has been sorely lacking.[61]

The theory and practice of counterinsurgency enjoyed their heyday under President Kennedy. His administration not only popularized the "Green Berets" but established the Office of Public Safety in 1962 to train foreign police as a buffer against urban insurgents. OPS encouraged foreign police to expand beyond their traditional role to embrace paramilitary, counterinsurgency and sophisticated intelligence functions. This police push was a Camelot experiment in containing domestic unrest before it reached the stage of guerrilla warfare. Washington also hoped through such training programs to guide "nation-building" in the Third World by exposing influential foreign security elites to American personnel, methods and institutions.[62]

As Attorney General Robert Kennedy told the first graduating class of the Washington, D.C.-based International Police Academy in 1964, "These are critical days for law enforcement... In the world today, most wars are 'police actions.' Law enforcement officials are a very real first line of defense, and the fate of governments and nations hangs in the balance."[63]

Up through 1974, when Congress disbanded the OPS, it trained more than 10,700 police officers from 77 countries in the United States and another million more abroad. Its courses ranged from crowd control to coping "with high level violence brought about by externally supported subversion, guerrilla activities in rural areas, and warfare." It also ran a camp with the CIA to instruct police in the art of building bombs and assassination devices.[64]

Proud OPS officials boasted that as of 1972 they had trained the heads of 13 foreign police forces, taught police from Nicaragua to Uruguay to "identify and apprehend urban terrorists" and boosted by 50 percent the size of the paramilitary Thai Border Patrol Police—a notoriously corrupt unit, as we shall see.[65]

But legislators saw matters differently. Horror stories of the OPS-financed prison "tiger cages" in South Vietnam and widespread torture committed by police states in South America and prompted Congress in 1974 to prohibit foreign police assistance—except for combatting the drug traffic.[66] A small enough loophole, that might have seemed. But it proved large enough to drive much of the old OPS program through.

OPS had long had responsibility for specialized narcotics enforcement training and support, though such activities had previously been a small part of its mission. Taking up the slack after 1973 was the State Department's International Narcotics Control program.

INC has supplied foreign governments with all manner of aid, including shotguns, submachine guns, jeeps, night vision devices, helicopters and communications equipment. Much of it has gone to ruthless dictatorships in such countries as Bolivia, Paraguay, Chile and Argentina—the very countries whose abuses had moved Congress to limit police aid in the first place.

In 1975 the Senate Appropriations Committee complained that "it is not the purpose of the narcotics program to give the participating government access to a continuous supply of free police equipment, much of which is possibly being used for purposes unrelated to control of drug traffic."[67]

A General Accounting Office study the next year confirmed the committee's worst fears, citing "circumstances that we believe are contrary to the intent of the prohibitions limiting assistance to foreign police." These included a six-fold increase in INC commodity assistance from fiscal years 1973 to 1974, and the fact that "commodities previously furnished to police units under the public safety program are now being provided to the same units under the narcotics program"—amounting to a blatant end run around Congress.[68]

Along with the equipment came advisers. The GAO pointed out that "Overseas narcotics advisers perform essentially the same functions that public safety advisers used to perform." Nothing had changed; as of 1978, former OPS officials staffed all INC posts in Latin America.[69]

Narcotics training programs filled the gap left by the demise of the Washington D.C.-based International Police Academy. INC funded the training of 11,763 foreign police between 1973 and 1976 alone. Courses continued to emphasize such topics as intelligence, surveillance and interrogation; many graduates of the DEA's Advanced International School applied their new expertise in lines of police work other than drug control.[70]

As in the Kennedy era, U.S. policy makers are chiefly interested in the ancillary benefits of such training programs. Besides "exposing...key visitors to United States agencies and procedures," said one State Department officer in 1981, they develop "personal ties of communication and cooperation between United States and foreign government officials."[71]

Narcotics training also serves key intelligence objectives, the DEA says, by creating a "brotherhood of foreign police officers who cooperate with each other in conducting investigations and exchange information regularly"—an unexceptional goal in theory, but chilling in the context of Third World realities.[72]

As Amnesty International and other human rights groups have documented, torture remains a regular, institutionalized practice in close to 100 countries throughout the world. The United States may not approve such practices, but the police it trains and the equipment it supplies under the narcotics program are often essential tools of police repression against dissident students, labor leaders and politicians. In Bolivia, as already noted, a U.S.-trained drug enforcement unit even staged an abortive coup in June 1984 against the democratic regime of President Siles Zuazo.[73]

In short, under the guise of drug enforcement, the United States continues to advance the original missions of police assistance: counterinsurgency, countersubversion and indirect political control.

ARGENTINA

A classic case of narcotics assistance serving repressive political ends rather than its stated purpose occurred during the mid-1970s in Argentina. There the INC commodity budget zoomed from $3,000 in fiscal 1973 to $347,000 in fiscal 1974, filling the vacuum left by the phasing out of OPS. The jump coincided with the October 1973 return from exile of Juan Peron, who brought with him a former policeman and Rasputin-like confidant, Jose Lopez Rega. Lopez Rega supervised the police from his new post as Minister of Social Welfare.

In March 1974, the State Department requested $200,000 for fiscal 1975 narcotics assistance and announced that $295,000 still clogged in the pipeline from past years would be spent in the next 18 months for vehicles, aircraft, communications and photographic equipment.

Two months later, Lopez Rega appeared in a nationally televised press conference with the U.S. ambassador to announce, "We hope to wipe out the drug traffic in Argentina. We have caught guerrillas after attacks who were high on drugs. Guerrillas are the main users of drugs in Argentina. Therefore the antidrug campaign will automatically be an antiguerrilla campaign as well."[74]

That neat formula would become a standard operating procedure of foreign leaders: Implicate the enemy in drug crimes, then collect U.S. police aid without any unpleasant questions from Washington.

The consequences in Argentina weren't long in coming. In May 1974, one month after Lopez Rega took delivery of automatic weapons and other equipment from INC, the Argentine Anticommunist Alliance, a shadowy death squad formed under his direction, began a prolonged campaign of assassination with the murder of a leftist priest.[75] Composed in part of off-duty police, the AAA likely benefited from training, communications and transportation equipment provided by the U.S. taxpayer.

Lopez Rega fled the country in the fall of 1975 after Argentina's Congress pinned dozens of political murders on him. Soon military intelligence sources were leaking allegations about Lopez Rega's own responsibility for the drug traffic: Cocaine, it seemed, had been a main underpinning of his secret empire. Lopez Rega was reportedly tied in with notorious smugglers high in the Paraguayan regime.[76]

The military coup of March 1976 strengthened the hand of security forces that already had their hands deep into the drug traffic. Lopez Rega's charge of guerrilla involvement in drug smuggling proved opportune for Argentina's new rulers. In February 1977, the junta's foreign minister declared war against subversion: "We attack its body through the war against guerrillas, and its spirit through the war against the drug traffic, both carriers of nihilistic and collectivist ideas."[77]

COLOMBIA

Responding to Colombia's national emergency following the murder of Senator Galan by the drug mafia in August 1989, the Bush administration did not send economic aid to subsidize crop substitution or raise the salaries of corruption-prone government officials. Instead it handed over $65 million in emergency *military* aid. This emphasis reflects Washington's true priorities in the region.

More than a decade ago, U.S. drug enforcement functionaries began spearheading a drive to turn Colombia into an armed camp. Following a helicopter tour of the Guajira Pensinsula in 1978, DEA Administrator Peter Bensinger urged the military to occupy the region, citing the marijuana industry as a "national security" threat to the nation. His words caused a storm of nationalist protest—but President Julio Turbay Ayala took Bensinger's advice and placed the entire peninsula under martial law—possibly to counter reports leaked from Washington that implicated him in the drug traffic. With $2.4 million in special U.S. funds, 6,500 soldiers swept through the wild area—to little practical effect against the big traffickers.[78]

At the same time, a presidential decree handed the military special authority against kidnappers, instigators of illegal strikes and other "social crimes." Some Supreme Court justices called the new regime a "constitutional dictatorship."[79] Most of the arrestees were held on subversion charges, not for drug crimes. Critics charged that military investigators relied extensively on torture.[8]

Pleased with the military's vigor, Washington proposed extending martial law elsewhere in the country. Joseph Linnemann, the State

Department's narcotics expert, exulted that "Involvement of the military's greater material and personnel resources has created the potential for similar campaigns in other regions of the country, such as the Llanos, the Choco, and along the southern border, all of which are real or potential producing or transit areas."[81]

Instead the army was withdrawn in December 1980 to stem rampant corruption within its ranks. But the military, with U.S. encouragement, remains a force in the anti-drug program precisely in order to pursue the anti-guerrilla fight. Like Lopez Rega in Argentina, Colombian security officials blame both subversion and drugs on the same "narco-guerrillas." As Defense Minster Gen. Gustavo Matamoros warned in 1984, "This alliance is a new threat to our democracy and we will continue to act rapidly and energetically to stop this danger."[82]

The military used such charges that year to undermine President Belisario Betancur's attempts to arrange a ceasefire with several guerrilla factions after he declared a state of emergency against the drug mafia. "The government said the state of siege was aimed at the traffickers and not at the guerrillas," one Colombian journalist explained, "but the army doesn't see it like that. As a result, we're now seeing the fiercest fighting between army and guerrillas in several years."[83]

The U.S. embassy in Bogota encouraged talk of a guerrilla-mafia alliance, thus sanctioning counterinsurgency under the guise of drug enforcement. Its briefing paper on the "FARC/Narc Connection" trumpeted alleged links between the Moscow-line Fuerzas Armada Revolucionarias de Colombia and wealthy cocaine producers.[84]

Impartial investigators acknowledge that FARC and several other Colombian guerrilla armies have dabbled in drugs to finance their operations. A GAO report declares that "as with other insurgent groups, FARC collects 'protection' payments from growers and traffickers in its operating territory, thus deriving the financial means to buy arms and others supplies." FARC may also "own and operate some cocaine laboratories," although it plays a small role in this sector of the business. But there is no solid evidence for allegations that left-wing guerrillas either guarded major cocaine processing installations or invaded the Colombian Supreme Court's Palace of Justice in 1985 on behalf of the drug lords.[85]

In fact, the "narco-terrorist" alliance is largely a myth. Marxist guerrillas despise the cowboy capitalism of the drug mafia bosses. The two groups are bloody business and ideological rivals, not allies.[86]

Even Nestor Sanchez, a former head of CIA operations in Latin America and Pentagon hardliner, admitted, "the drug traffickers today are trying to move away from the subversives...because they're interested in making money. They're not interested in ideologies or politics or anything like that, which sometimes interferes with their moneymaking schemes... Today we see in Colombia the narcotics traffickers...organizing and arming their own armies, trying to get away from the insurgents."[87]

As early as 1981, indeed, several notorious smugglers and their allies in the army set up a death squad targeted against the allies of guerrillas who kidnapped family members of the drug chiefs for ransom. "Muerte a Secuestradores" (MAS—Death to Kidnappers) went on to murder more than 300 suspected leftists.[88]

Since then, some 140 well-armed paramilitary organizations, financed by the drug mafia, have taken over from MAS to wage war against both leftist guerrillas and innocent civilians suspected of leftist sympathies. They call themselves the "Fascist Red Army," "Death to Revolutionaries of the Northeast," "Executioners," and, more neutral in name only, the "Association of Peasants and Cattle Ranchers of Middle Magdalena."

In 1983, Colombia's attorney general indicted 59 members of the military for links with MAS. Many of the accused later won promotions after the high command came to their defense. Since then, it has been clear that elements of the military had more interest in collaborating with the kings of cocaine against the left than in stamping out the drug trade. As a U.S. congressional staff report observed in 1989, "some members of the Colombian military may temporarily form alliances with traffickers to attack guerrillas..." Americas Watch put it more strongly: "There is compelling evidence that regional Army chiefs and high-ranking intelligence operatives are involved in facilitating the commission of atrocious acts by private [drug-financed] armies and death squads." In early 1990, President Virgilio Barco reportedly dismissed four generals suspected of going easy on the drug lords.[89]

Guerrillas aren't the only targets of that alliance. In November 1988, for example, a paramilitary squad entered the town of Segovia, rounded up inhabitants suspected of supporting the leftist Union Patriotica (UP) party. The invaders murdered them systematically, leaving 43 dead and more than 50 wounded. A judge in Medellin later ordered the arrest of an army colonel and three captains for the crime. "We have arrived at the conclusion that the paramilitary is the military and the military is the government," declared the party's president in early 1990, after a few dozen more activists had joined the several thousand UP victims of death squad violence.[90]

Typical also of military behavior was its September 1989 raid of the Medellin-based human rights organization, Instituto de Capacitacion Popular, and the arrest and torture of the center's director and other officers on the pretext of investigating drug trafficking.[91]

Corrupt elements of Colombia's army have no intention of going after the real traffickers. In July 1989, an army death squad reportedly murdered four people, trying without success to rub out a DEA informant. One of those responsible was allegedly the commander of the army's Special Urban Forces, who in turn enjoyed the defense minister's protection. Colombia's attorney general later warned that the drug barons had infiltrated the military's ranks in a big way. "It was a mistake to bring the Colombian army into this fight and to put it in touch with corruption," he declared. On another occasion he observed, "It is not for a lack of military might that the drug-trafficking barons have not yet been captured; they do not have unbeatable armies. It is because they have informants in the...Army who forewarn them about operations to capture them."[92]

Even so, the Bush administration budgeted more than $50 million in military aid to Colombia for fiscal year 1990, $60.5 million in 1991, and additional Export-Import Bank subsidies for military sales—all in the name of fighting drugs. U.S. military aid represents far and away the bulk of Washington's anti-narcotics assistance to Colombia, even though its national police has primary responsibility for drug enforcement.[93]

Given Colombian realities, such aid cannot help but promote counterinsurgency objectives over narcotics control. Indeed the State Department itself admitted in 1988, while asking Congress to give anti-drug aid to the Colombian military, that "the military is engaged in a day-to-day struggle with the guerrillas... This is a two-front war for Colombia and the division of labor has been that the military has taken the guerrilla front and the special anti-narcotics unit...has taken on the narcotics traffickers"[94]

American officials rationalize this aid with the crude and misleading narco-terrorist model. Ann Wrobleski, the State Department's top narcotics officer, testified in 1989 that Colombian defense officials told her that "when they hit a coke lab, they deny the guerrillas guns. And that's a very direct relationship. I think that the Colombian government has certainly come to the realization that what they have out there is not two separate groups, but two groups who certainly seem to cooperate more and more."[95]

By that same logic, however, the Colombian military may rationalize using U.S. drug aid to attack guerrillas or suspected civilian sympathizers. Spotty evidence suggests that is exactly what is happening. "Following a recent military offensive by the FARC" in January 1990, reported Coletta Youngers, an Andean expert at the Washington Office on Latin America, "the Colombian military strafed villages in Uraba, Yondo and Meta with helicopter artillery fire. Witnesses claim that the attacks were not aimed at guerrilla camps, as the military said, but at civilian settlements and that in some cases Blackhawk helicopters—provided to the Colombians by the U.S. government for antinarcotics operations—were used." In February, moreover, a military bombardment with American A-37 jets and helicopter gunships reportedly forced 1,400 peasant families to flee their homes.[96]

MEXICO

Once considered the classic success story of bilateral drug eradication, Mexico has demonstrated instead the consequences of giving U.S. aid to corrupt police and military who turned it against the peasantry.

During the 1970s, the critical decade of opium poppy and marijuana eradication, the INC program pumped more than $95 million into Mexico.[97] Aid included 64 helicopters, 24 airplanes, submachine and shotguns, tear gas projectiles, and at least 30 full-time DEA agents working in conjunction with the Federal Police.[98]

Critics have charged that narcotics enforcement was used as a pretext to crush peasant land occupations and peasant-worker alliances in the countryside. Some of the worst incidents occurred in the southern state of Guerrero, home of Acapulco Gold and poor dirt farmers who sheltered a modest guerrilla movement until the army stamped it out in 1974. "Guerrero today remains in a state of military occupation," one American journalist observed two years later, "and many of its people view the current campaign against drugs, carried out by Mexican soldiers and judicial police who march in from their own encampments or drop from helicopters, as a veneer of legitimacy for an ongoing campaign to terrorize the populace and keep down an incipient anti-government movement." The head of the State Judicial Police in northern Guerrero, meanwhile, was reportedly himself a heroin dealer.[99]

In early 1978, 7,000 Mexican soldiers backed by DEA advisers waged a "special war" against marijuana cultivators in the northern states of Durango, Sinaloa and Chihuahua. DFS had already relocated the main traffickers to Guadalajara, under its protection. The real targets of Operation Condor, according to reports from the U.S. Catholic Conference, were Indian peasants. Tanks and helicopters intimidated the local population; herbicide sprayings poisoned their land and starved them out.[100]

A six-month investigation of Federal Judicial Police practices in this operation, published by an American reporter in 1979, found that "torture, extortion, self-incrimination, forced confession, incommunicado detention and excessive detention without sentencing" were "regular practices." The worst incidents occurred in Sinaloa, where DEA agents coordinated field training and actual operations by their Mexican counterparts. Witnesses, including Mexican police, accused American agents of standing by during torture sessions. The Sinaloa Bar Association compiled no fewer than 567 prisoner affidavits attesting to torture in connection with "Operation Condor."

Victor Gomez Vidal, the highest ranking state security official in Sinaloa, charged that "Operation Condor is a way for some federal authorities to make themselves very rich. They have their own jail—nobody knows who comes and goes but them. It's a closed system. And once inside they torture people to see who has the money and who doesn't and it's their word against ours." When the notoriously brutal commander of the federal police was gunned down in late 1978, he left an estate valued at $10 million.[101]

A similar fate befell a prominent Mexican journalist, Roberto Martinez Montenegro, who covered the explosive growth of Mexico's drug trade from Culiacan, capital of Sinaloa. His daring reporting put numerous high-ranking law enforcement and government officials behind bars, including the former head of the state police. Above all, he attacked Condor as a fraud, aimed not at the drug lords but at attacking the peasantry. Assassinated in February 1978, he was smeared in death as a criminal extortionist by no less than Miguel Nazar Haro, who would soon become notorious as the drug-trafficking chief of DFS (see Chapter IV).[102]

Such repression continued into the 1980s. The war on drugs still serves as a convenient weapon against suspected subversives, human rights activists, journalists, opposition political leaders and entire communities of Indians. The national drug emergency has given the official perpetrators of crimes against these groups a name: "the untouchables."[103] One of their most significant victims in 1990 appears to have been Norma Corona Sapien, lawyer and president of the independent Human Rights Commission of Sinaloa.[104]

In a report issued in June 1990, Americas Watch cited Mexico's lawless brand of drug enforcement as one cause of the upsurge in popular concern over human rights:

To combat drug trafficking, the Federal Judicial Police have appointed an elite squad of officers, many of whom formerly served in earlier incarnations of repressive public security units, and are widely reputed to be corrupted by involvement in or covering up of drug trafficking. The squad enjoys unhindered freedom to locate and destroy drugs and arrest those participating in drug trafficking, and operates with near absolute impunity. Federal narcotics police are accountable for a large number of cases of murder, torture, and abuse of process in Mexico today... The blatant nature of these atrocities, combined with the fact that under the pretext of drug investigations many of Mexico's middle and upper class families are experiencing treatment previously reserved for the more anonymous poor, has led to an increase in publicity about human rights abuses.[105]

Responding to the public outcry, President Salinas ordered the lifting of police drug roadblocks, banned the use by police of unmarked cars seized from criminals and curbed other security force activities in order to prevent human rights violations.[106]

PERU

The U.S. push for narcotics enforcement in Peru, as in Mexico, has evolved into a counterinsurgency campaign. The main targets in this case are the fanatical Maoist guerrillas of Sendero Luminoso.

In the early 1980s, the United States began training and equipping an anti-drug police unit based in Tingo Maria, a center of the coca growing region northeast of Lima. The police began conducting joint operations with the air force and counterinsurgency-trained civil guard.[107]

A series of devastating guerrilla raids, including police station bombings, forced a cancellation of police field operations. The *New York Times* reported in August 1984 that with drug programs shut down "the strike force is now almost fully occupied in the counterinsurgency campaign. This new role has raised questions among United States officials in Peru and in Washington about the spending of United States Government funds that are earmarked for narcotics control, not for counterinsurgency."[108]

Although Sendero guerrillas do garner tens of millions of dollars each year from taxing the coca trade, U.S. officials admit there is little evidence of a close alliance between the smugglers and the guerrillas.[109] Peru's security forces use the drug issue as an excuse to go after the greater danger. In July 1984 President Fernando Belaunde Terry declared a "holy war" against what he called the "narcotics-terrorism threat," extending a state of national emergency for 30 days to give the armed forces a chance to use "new methods" against the guerrillas.[110]

The army, however, did not see narcos and guerrillas as allies. It shut down anti-drug police operations and enlisted traffickers in the war against Sendero. "We have to have popular support to fight terrorism," one officer said. "We have to have a friend in the population. You can't do that by eradicating coca."[111]

The army has returned to the Upper Huallaga Valley—and so has the counterinsurgency campaign. U.S. personnel are even joining the fight against Sendero. In early 1990, Shining Path guerrillas attacked the main anti-drug base at Santa Lucia in the Upper Huallaga Valley. U.S. helicopter pilots took to the air in Huey gunships for a two-hour battle to beat them off. To plan and carry out its operations in the region, the DEA has teamed up with the Pentagon's Center for Low Intensity Conflict, a classic counterinsurgency outfit.[11]

In early 1990, the Bush administration announced plans to deliver $35 million in military aid, under the anti-drug program, to combat Sendero directly. The money would finance a large military training base in the heart of the Upper Huallaga Valley, staffed by Special Forces counterinsurgency trainers; six army battalions; and refurbishing of 20 A-37 jets. Melvyn Levitsky, the State Department's top narcotics officer, explained, "We have to up the capability to hit the Sendero, to provide a cover—a security cover for the operations by the police and the military against the drug traffickers."[113]

That rationale falls apart under examination. Sending aid to the Peruvian military in the name of fighting drugs is almost a contradiction in terms. Levitsky himself admitted that widespread reports of military corruption "have ranged from taking payoffs from the traffickers so that they could go after the Sendero, that is to let the [drug] flights in, to other kinds of collusion."[114]

Top military officers have made no secret about halting drug eradication efforts in order to win peasant support against the guerrillas—just as they did in 1984-1985. General Alberto Arciniega, the army's field commander in the Upper Huallaga Valley until 1990, said, "The magnitude of the problems we face is far greater than narcotics. My order is: Nobody must touch the campesino coca grower. This doesn't mean I support drug trafficking." He might as well, though. "We hit laboratories," said one senior US embassy official, "but there are no arrests, no seizures. It's just harrassment. We're not making major progress here." As a result, coca fields have expanded and drug shipments are picking up.[115]

Worse yet, the Peruvian military only fuels the insurgency by brutalizing the peasantry. The State Department's own annual report on human rights around the globe blamed government security forces for more than 500 forced disappearances in 1989, a world record that year. According to Juan Mendez, executive director of Americas Watch, army units sometimes react to ambushes and attacks "by invading a community and killing dozens of young and old males, sometimes in full view of relatives." In addition, right-wing death squads linked to the army "have targeted journalists, lawyers and human right monitors," bombing the headquarters of no fewer than three rights organizations in Lima in one week. The most prominent of these death squads, the

Rodrigo Franco Front, was reportedly financed by funds that police confiscated in narcotics raids.[116]

Sending more military aid to Peru—a project jeopardized by the breakdown of U. S. talks with the government of Alberto Fujimori in September 1990—would put counterinsurgency ahead of all other political and economic priorities. In Peru's unstable situation, bolstering a military that held total power from 1968 to 1980 can only shift the balance of forces in favor of an institution whose loyalties to democracy, human rights and civilian rule are tenuous at best.

BURMA

Opium production in the Golden Triangle is concentrated in the wild Shan states of northeastern Burma. The poppy crop, high in value but low in weight, is well suited for transport over rugged mountain terrain.

Opium has become the financial mainstay of several separatist political movements in the Shan states, which rebelled against Rangoon in the late 1950s. "It's like a cottage industry," said one guerrilla commander. "Every army has its own lab at the border (of Thailand), just like homes in Europe used to have their own ovens to bake bread. We take care of our own needs... We must fight the Rangoon government and we must have weapons."[117]

Some of these groups are really freebooting smuggling gangs with only a thin nationalist veneer; others have a genuine political agenda. Of the latter, the Burmese Communist Party controls the largest opium poppy-growing territory. In the early 1970s the BCP encouraged crop substitution.[118] After China cut back its support later in the decade, however, the BCP took up opium smuggling and even heroin refining.[119]

But long before the BCP began dealing opium, U.S. and Burmese authorities targeted it and other rebel groups for suppression under the guise of drug enforcement. Rangoon tolerated and even armed several large-scale, anti-communist traffickers until they developed political ambitions of their own.[120] But it cracked down mercilessly on the real Shan nationalists.

American support to the Burmese police included 28 helicopters, 6 fixed-wing transport planes, 5 herbicide-spraying aircraft, communications equipment, and associated training and support.[121] In a letter to Rep. Lester Wolff in 1977, Lt. Gen. Bo Mya, commander-in-chief of the Karen National Liberation Army, charged that

The helicopters given to the Burmese...Government for use in Narcotic Suppression is nothing but a farce and a misused gift of honor. Over a month old fighting in Wankha a place on the Burma-Thailand border was a good proof. Not a poppy was or is grown in the area. They used helicopter you have given them as a combat transport. This kind of method has been adopted not to the Karen Freedom Fighter alone, but to all the Kachin, Shan, Men, Kayah etc., the minority groups who are fighting for their freedom as we are. (sic)[122]

Wolff's House narcotics committee reported "convincing evidence that Burma's anti-narcotics campaign is a form of economic warfare aimed at the subjugation of its minority peoples... A policy which encourages attacks on farmers, the destruction of fields and livestock, and the contemplated use of herbicides is incompatible with any civilized conception of human rights..."[123]

In recent years, Asia Watch and other human rights groups have documented the use of U.S.-supplied herbicides to starve rebellious national minority groups. University of California ethnographer Bernard Nietschmann commented in 1987, "Burma's ability to expand its wars was made possible by United States weapons, aircraft and very toxic herbicides supplied to Rangoon to eradicate opium poppies. Ne Win's Government is using drug war weaponry to fight territorial and insurgent wars. Instead of spraying opium poppies with herbicides, the Burmese Air Force is spraying villages and food crops to weaken civilian support of armed resistance."[124]

In the late 1970s, and again a decade later, opium-trafficking Shan forces proposed a detente: The United States could simply buy from them the entire opium crop, some 250 tons with a street value estimated by the DEA at $16 billion, for a mere $6 million to $12 million. There was even a precedent in the U.S. purchase of 26 tons of opium from the KMT for $1 million in 1972.[125]

The reasons given by the State Department for opposing the idea highlighted the politics of the entire international narcotics control program: A preëmptive buy would "work directly counter to our foreign policy objectives in that area" by aiding separatist parties and even "Communist insurgencies against the friendly governments of Burma and Thailand."[126] The unspoken corollary was that assistance to central government paramilitary narcotics units would serve U.S. foreign policy interests by undermining those same insurgencies.

It is hard to believe any other policy ever drove U.S. narcotics aid to Burma. Certainly Washington cannot have really believed the Rangoon regime would ever stamp out drugs. Drug corruption has long permeated every level of the military and police. The ruling military lends trains, trucks, airplanes and naval vessels to privileged smugglers and guards their shipments; in 1988, Kachin rebels claimed to have seized more than two tons of opium from a government military unit in north central Burma. For years, the military has permitted the biggest drug lord of all, Chan Chi-fu (Khun Sa), to move his multi-hundred-ton opium loads in return for organizing Shan militias to crack down on ethnic and Communist insurgents. And in early 1990, the regime began supplying weapons and food to the United Wa State Army, a notorious heroin-trafficking group.[127]

The country's longtime military ruler, Ne Win, and his vice president, Aye Ko, were widely believed to share in kickbacks from drug syndicates protected by the military. "In fact," declared Sen. Daniel Moynihan of New York in August 1988, "in Ne Win perhaps we have been dealing with an Asian Noriega."[128]

A month later, Burma's military leaders brutally crushed pro-democracy demonstrators and greatly stepped up their murderous suppression of ethnic resistance. Before long they began forcing hundreds of thousands of citizens from the cities. Widespread reports of violent government repression moved Washington to cut off further anti-drug assistance, including herbicides. The State Department, reflecting Washington's disapproval, belatedly admits that the regime "has a sort of collusive relationship with some of the traffickers, and is allowing them in some kind of bargained way to go ahead unfettered." Drug production is indeed booming, up 50 percent between 1988 and 1990. But the DEA reportedly still argues for resuming official cooperation in order to return to the country.[129]

The wholesale provision of counterinsurgency aid disguised as anti-drug assistance has done untold damage to America's image as a beacon of justice abroad. And by turning drug enforcement into an instrument of social repression, Washington has also done untold damage to the legitimacy of its efforts to control narcotics in the source countries.

Chapter III

Narcotics and Communism

The dreaded 'heroin epidemic' of 1969 and 1970, along with the rise of recreational drug use throughout the 1960s, drove millions of voters into the law-and-order camp by giving them a bogeyman far more virulent, despicable and immediate than the classical godless communist of yore: the pusher... It was the answer to a central dilemma: the exhaustion of the cold war.

—Robert Singer[130]

Hostile governments, no less than hostile insurgencies, have long been targets of U.S. drug policy. Against such governments, the drug issue has become a significant propaganda weapon, a rationale for U.S.-sponsored destabilization campaigns abroad and the mobilization of public opinion at home.

The popular image of Communist subversion—its poisoning of minds with enticing propaganda—has a counterpart in the image of the drug pusher enslaving America's youth with alluring poisons of the body. Both entail a fall from grace, a loss of reason and will, a disruption of social bonds.

Viewed this way, narcotics enforcement is an essential element of the nation's defense against hostile attempts to undermine the physical and moral strength of our population. As President Ford once declared, "All nations of the world—friend and adversary alike—must understand that America considers the illegal export of opium to the country a threat to our national security."[131]

Harry Anslinger, who led the Federal Bureau of Narcotics from its founding in 1930 until 1962, championed this outlook. "Reefers and propaganda," he declared, "...go hand in hand." He warned Americans to "be on guard against the use of drugs as a political weapon by the

Communists" who "may try to make narcotics a new 'sixth' column to weaken and destroy selected targets in the drive for world domination."[132]

His favorite bete noir was "Red China," which he accused of planning a "long range dope-and-dialectic assault on America and its leaders." Some of the earliest charges against that regime seem to have come from Gen. Douglas MacArthur's right-wing military intelligence chief, Charles Willoughby, and from a CIA-funded labor organization. Anslinger forever talked about "Communist" morphine, even though his own agent in Bangkok—sent to preëmpt the Customs Service from opening a post there ahead of the FBN—referred to the Nationalist Chinese 93rd Army, expelled from China to Burma in 1949, as the main source of Southeast Asian heroin.[133]

Anslinger never let facts get in the way of his political case. Consider the publicity surrounding a San Francisco drug bust in January 1959. The agent in charge called it "the biggest Chinese narcotics operation that we've ever come across." Anslinger later cited it as proof that "Red China" was the primary source of heroin entering the United States. Buried in news accounts was the fact that one of the ring leaders was an official of the Chinese Anti-Communist Committee, whom U.S. officials permitted to flee to Taiwan.[134]

Fourteen years later, when a large bust in New York City turned up a plastic bag of pure heroin labelled (in English) "People's Republic of China," Washington didn't bite. A State Department spokesman remarked drily, "there would seem to be a potential for counterfeit here."[135]

What had happened in the interim, besides Anslinger's retirement, was the opening to China and the start of an American effort to bring it into the anti-Soviet camp.

Political expediency governed Washington's public position on Chinese complicity in the drug traffic. Thus as late as 1970 the BNDD stated flatly that "opium is cultivated in vast quantities in the Yunnan Province of China." Yet by 1971, following President Nixon's announcement of his forthcoming mission to China, the State Department was claiming "There is no reliable evidence that the Communist Chinese have *ever* engaged in or sanctioned the illicit export of opium or its derivatives." (Emphasis added.) Indeed, the White

House instructed executive agencies to beware of Communist dope stories, alleging that they originated in the propaganda mills of Taiwan.[136]

Despite the reversal on China, the Communist-drug connection remained a potent propaganda theme against the Soviets' "evil empire." Secretary of State George Shultz, pointing to "the complicity of some Communist governments in the drug trade," charged in 1984 that "smuggling massive amounts of drugs into Western nations may serve their broader goal of attempting to weaken the fabric of Western democratic society."[137]

Some Communist regimes, and many insurgent movements of all political stripes, unquestionably deal in drugs. Bulgaria had a particularly notorious reputation for heroin smuggling, money laundering and arms trafficking. The Laotian government may have tolerated heroin production as well. Marxist FARC guerrillas in Colombia, Sikh terrorists in India, and militant Tamil separatists in Sri Lanka are among the many movements that put ends before means.[138]

Drugs know no ideology. But there is little evidence for the insidious special motives imputed to leftist regimes by conservative critics.

The Reagan White House, preoccupied with stemming the spread of Soviet influence in Central America and the Caribbean, repeatedly alleged Cuban and Nicaraguan complicity in drug smuggling to bolster public support for its roll-back policies.

In July 1984, for example, Reagan administration officials—possibly Oliver North himself—leaked to the conservative *Washington Times* lurid stories linking top Nicaraguan leaders to notorious Colombian cocaine traffickers. Among those allegedly implicated by a DEA sting were Interior Minister Tomas Borge and Defense Minister Humberto Ortega.[139]

Opponents of the Sandinista regime—who never raised a peep of protest about major drug links of either the Somoza regime or the Contras—milked the charges for all they were worth. The 1984 GOP presidential platform condemned "the Sandinista government's smuggling of illegal drugs into the United States as a crime against American society and international law." Sen. Paula Hawkins, R-FL, whose constituents included large numbers of anti-Communist Cuban exiles, said "It is not enough for them to maim a generation of American children, for they use the blood money from their drug sales to create mayhem throughout the Western hemisphere." American cocaine users, she insisted, "must realize that they are tools in a geopolitical movement designed to perpetuate totalitarianism in Nicaragua and to spread Marxist insurgency throughout Latin America."[140]

Testimony from former participants in the drug trade supports the view that some Nicaraguan officials, like officials of every other Central American country, may have been corrupted. A U.S. indictment of Colombian cartel leaders claims that in 1984 they brought 1,400 kilos of cocaine into Nicaragua, storing it at the Los Brasiles Air Force Base. According to Floyd Carlton, a Panamanian pilot active in the drug trade, the Medellin Cartel actually planned to build a large cocaine lab in Nicaragua to replace a production complex lost in Colombia.[141]

But was this a case of common state corruption or a political decision by the Sandinistas to exploit a new source of revenue and undermine America's youth? Or was the whole affair a set-up? Pablo Escobar, a leader of the Medellin Cartel, allegedly asked an associate "to explore the possibility of starting drug-related operations in Nicaragua, documenting them, and then using the information to bargain with the United States for amnesty." Cartel leaders wanted to "work for American intelligence...thereby incurring amnesty for their efforts," according to the DEA. These devious motives may explain why one Nicaraguan government official supposedly implicated by a DEA sting was based in a house the U.S. embassy rented continuously from 1985, if not before.[142]

Owing to the politically inspired White House leak, the world does not yet know how deeply drug corruption penetrated the Sandinista regime. The DEA's sting fell apart just when it promised to net the Medellin Cartel's top leadership. But DEA officials admitted having little evidence to implicate Sandinista leaders. Stanley Marcus, the U.S. attorney in Miami who indicted one former Nicaraguan official on cocaine charges, also confessed the weakness of administration claims against the regime. And by 1988, DEA Administrator John Lawn was willing to describe Nicaragua as largely untouched by drugs.[143]

Within a year or two of its founding, the Castro regime, too, became the target of narcotics-related propaganda, some of it downright preposterous. For example, anti-Castro sources claimed that Fidel Castro personally discussed guns-for-drugs trades with Jack Ruby, the Dallas killer of Lee Harvey Oswald.[144]

In 1976 a Cuban exile leader, Manuel de Armas, who defected to Havana after working for the CIA, declared that his former employer was planning to blacken Cuba's image with disinformation linking the Communist government to drugs. But his credibility can hardly be taken for granted.[145]

Cuba certainly has not avoided the corrupting influence of this worldwide trade. Throughout much of the 1970s, U.S. prosecutors and drug agents heard from reliable informants that Havana was taking a share of profits in return for providing traffickers a haven and transfer station for drug shipments originating in Colombia. In 1982, admittedly on rather shaky evidence, a federal grand jury in Miami indicted four senior Cuban officials and 10 others of conspiring "to use Cuba as a loading station and source of supplies for ships transporting" Quaaludes and marijuana to the southeastern United States.[146]

The DEA assistant special agent-in-charge of the case emphasized, "We are not saying this is the policy of the Cuban government. We don't know and we have not suggested there is a conspiracy by the Cuban government in general." The State Department's top narcotics officer similarly cautioned that "there is no solid evidence of Cuban Government involvement, nor do reports confirm a connection between international terrorism and Cuban involvement in narcotics trafficking."[147]

Revelations in yet another Miami case implicating high Cuban officials prompted the Castro regime in June 1989 to arrest, try and execute a highly decorated general and ranking members of the Interior Ministry on charges of smuggling tons of cocaine through Cuba for the Medellin Cartel.[148] At least one of the trafficking conspiracies grew out of Havana's official, if covert, program to circumvent the American embargo. Once again the question arises: How high up did the conspiracy go? Cuban leaders professed shock and betrayal. Many skeptical analysts, on the other hand, assume Castro simply had political reasons to do away with his partners in crime. The fact that fugitive financier and drug trafficker Robert Vesco has for years enjoyed refuge in Cuba indicates that Castro cannot be entirely unwitting about his country's protection of smuggling.[149]

The truth in these matters is much murkier than some partisans allow. But serious drug experts agree that whatever Communist-drug connection does exist has little impact on the availability of drugs in the United States.[150] And it is equally clear is that outrage over foreign complicity in the drug trade has been highly selective. U.S. politicians have been quick to exploit the issue as an emotional vehicle for pursuing other agendas. The deep and tragic irony is that Washington itself has done as much as any government to promote the growth of the world drug trade.

Chapter IV

Narcotics Enforcement and the CIA

You can't buy, stock or transport drugs unless you have protection in political and administrative circles. The most useful sort is to be found half-way up the ladder, especially in the army, police and customs where the pay's bad and ambitions are unlimited. High-up officials have less need to help themselves along by breaking the law; but then, of course, a good few of them have got where they are because, at some stage or other of their career, they've made a bundle out of corrupt deals. Best of all is the protection given by the [intelligence] outfits who can save you no end of trouble. I've often flown their agents on secret missions of one kind or another. In return they'd wink at my other trips.

—Corsican ex-trafficker[151]

They [the CIA] have a tough job to do. They are not necessarily dealing with the angels of the world, and we can't really object when they end up rubbing elbows with some of the dregs of the world.
—Rtd. Adm. Daniel Murphy, Vice President Bush's top drug aide[152]

I am absolutely convinced that we have...had various branches of our government—CIA, etc.—who have operated, who have worked with drug traffickers for various geopolitical reasons, etc. That is absolutely intolerable.
—Senator Alphonse D'Amato, R-NY[153]

We gave up the drug war in favor of a war against Communism. In fact, we made a conscious choice.
—Former senior DEA agent Michael Levine[154]

The CIA is a relative newcomer to the drug enforcement field. It only joined the drug war in 1969, by order of President Nixon. Under President Bush, its newly formed Counternarcotics Center has become the central clearinghouse for international drug intelligence. A classified memorandum of understanding between the DEA and CIA gives CIA primary responsibility for the use of foreign drug informants.[155]

Knowledgeable drug enforcement agents reportedly grumble about the CIA's "past lack of interest and present ineffectiveness" in the battle against drugs.[156] Some DEA officials are no doubt simply jealous of their bureaucratic turf. Those with longer memories, however, have good reason to wonder just whose side the CIA is really on.

The CIA was "present at the creation" of most of the major post-World War II drug production centers and trafficking syndicates. Its material support and political protection nurtured the great heroin and cocaine empires whose power today rivals that of many governments. Without critical American aid they might have remained limited, regional gangs; with it, they forged truly international production and smuggling networks.

Successful trafficking organizations require more than organizational skill, financial sophistication and ruthlessness. Above all, they need political or police protection. The route to market domination lies in corrupting political leaders and serving ambitious law enforcement authorities by trading information on competitors for protection from arrest. The same rule holds true for successful international drug syndicates. On that level, the Central Intelligence Agency has offered unmatched opportunities for protection. Its marriage of convenience with underworld organizations to advance Washington's political agendas abroad fostered the rise of notorious syndicates in Sicily, Marseilles, Southeast Asia, Mexico, Central America and Afghanistan.

From the Sicilian Mafia to the Corsican Brotherhood

The CIA's parent and sister organizations, the Office of Strategic Services (OSS) and Office of Naval Intelligence (ONI), cultivated the leaders of the Italian Mafia—one of the great drug syndicates of all times—during World War II. Earl Brennan, head of OSS intelligence for the Italian Mediterranean theater, recruited heavily from the New York and Chicago underworlds and kept in touch with Sicilian Mafia leaders exiled by Italian dictator Benito Mussolini. OSS operatives not only freed Mafia leaders from Sicilian prisons and conspired with them to suppress the burgeoning Italian Communist Party but even toyed for a while with Mafia-sponsored plans to secede from the rest of Italy.[157]

The Navy's collaboration with gangsters was, if anything, even more sinister. ONI in effect legitimized much of the New York City underworld by allying with imprisoned Mafia boss Charles "Lucky" Luciano—ostensibly to use his criminal army to prevent sabotage on Eastern seabord ports and gain intelligence on Sicily prior to the allied landing. At the height of the partnership, the navy assigned 155 officers and enlisted men to operations involving continuous liaison with such hoodlums as Luciano, Meyer Lansky, Joe Adonis, and Frank Costello. In practice, this arrangement netted the U.S. government relatively little information of practical wartime value. It gave the Mafia, however, a convenient excuse to crush its rivals in the union movement with government sanction.[158]

These alliances had longterm effects, both criminal and political. Luciano's wartime services to the Navy won him a pardon from New York Governor Thomas Dewey, who had prosecuted the gangster years earlier. Deported to Italy, Luciano proceeded to build an enormous heroin empire. First he diverted supplies from the legal market; then he developed connections in Lebanon and Turkey that supplied morphine base to labs in Sicily and Marseilles.[159]

Politically, this same alliance cemented the control of corrupt but anti-communist Christian Democratic leaders in Sicily and southern Italy. Much blood flowed to achieve that goal; in 1947-48, U.S. intelligence officers allegedly helped the Mafia seize total power on the island by massacring several hundred leftists. Former CIA operative Miles Copeland claims that "had it not been for the Mafia the Communists would by now be in control of Italy."[160]

The CIA pursued much the same strategy in France. It sent funds to the heroin-smuggling Corsican underworld of Marseilles to assist its battle with Communist unions for control of the city's docks in 1947. (The CIA's top Corsican agent in that struggle was reportedly implicated in a massive opium smuggling ring from Laos into Vietnam in the mid-1960s.) By 1951, the Corsicans and Luciano had pooled their forces to dominate the heroin market.[161] Corsican master chemists would dominate the world heroin trade until the breaking of the "French Connection" in the early 1970s.

Rise of the Golden Triangle

Along with these two pillars of the post-World War II heroin market, the CIA helped establish a third in the "Golden Triangle," the mountainous border region of Laos, Burma, Thailand and China's Yunnan Province where opium poppies grow in astonishing abundance.

During World War II, in China as in Sicily, the OSS and Navy worked closely with gangster elements who controlled vast supplies of opium, morphine and heroin. The boss of this trade, a longstanding ally of Nationalist leader Chiang Kai-shek, directed his enormous army of followers to cooperate closely with American intelligence—though his patriotism did not stop him from trading with the Japanese.[162]

His heroin empire folded after the victory of the Chinese Communist revolution in 1949. But a new one emerged after Nationalist (KMT) forces under the command of General Li Mi fled from Yunnan into the wild Shan States of eastern Burma. By 1951, if not earlier, they began receiving arms, ammunition and other supplies via CIA airlift to facilitate their abortive efforts to rekindle an anticommunist resistance in China. Repelled from China with heavy losses, the KMT settled down with the local population to organize and expand the lucrative opium trade from Burma and northern Thailand. In this endeavor, they continued to enjoy support both from the CIA and its "assets" in the Thai military and police, who convoyed the drugs to Thai ports. By 1972, the KMT controlled fully 80 percent of the Golden Triangle's enormous opium trade.[163]

The CIA's relationship to these drug merchants—and to corrupt Laotian, Thai and Vietnamese political and military leaders—attracted little attention until the early 1970s. As early as 1966, however, Harrison Salisbury noted the rise of heroin production in the region and added: "There are skeptics who feel that not a few recipients of the bounty of U.S. aid and the CIA may have a deeper interest in the opium business than in Communist business. In the center of the whole trade is a hardy band of Chinese Nationalist troops who were flown to China's Yunnan province border years ago in one of the early CIA operations... They have managed to turn a pretty penny in poppies."[164]

In 1970, a correspondent for the *Christian Science Monitor* reported, "Clearly the CIA is cognizant of, if not party to, the extensive movement of opium out of Laos. One charter pilot told me that 'friendly' opium shipments get special CIA clearance and monitoring on their flights southward out of the country." A California congressman even charged that "clandestine yet official operations of the United States government could be aiding and abetting heroin traffic here at home."[165] And not just at home: By the end of 1970, 30,000 American servicemen in Vietnam were addicted to heroin.

But the full story did not break until 1972, when Yale University doctoral candidate Alfred McCoy published his trailblazing study, *The Politics of Heroin in Southeast Asia.* The CIA's efforts to quash the book brought McCoy's expose national publicity and only strengthened his thesis: that Cold War politics and American covert operations had fostered a heroin boom in the Golden Triangle.[166]

Hoping to undercut McCoy's evidence, the CIA's Inspector General undertook a major field investigation of the charges. The secret IG report predictably cleared the agency of having "sanctioned or supported drug trafficking as a matter of policy"—a claim McCoy never made. But the report did express "concern" over "agents and local officials with whom we are in contact who have been or may be still involved in one way or another in the drug business... What to do about these people is a particularly troublesome problem, in view of its implications for some of our operations, particularly in Laos." Noting that the CIA did not interfere with the "tribals" who raised opium lest they refuse to "cooperate," the report admitted, "The war has clearly been our overriding priority in Southeast Asia and all other issues have taken second place in the scheme of things. It would be foolish to deny this, and we see no reason to do so."[167]

The scandal touched off by McCoy's book produced not only blanket official denials, but also contradictory assurances that Washington's priorities had changed since President Nixon declared his "war on drugs." The evidence strongly suggests otherwise.

Based on privileged access to DEA sources, reporter Elaine Shannon has observed:

After the fall of South Vietnam, the CIA and the National Security Agency expanded their facilities in Bangkok and Chiang Mai in northern Thailand to monitor military and political activity in Vietnam, Laos, Southern China and northern Burma. The smugglers were natural allies. DEA agents who served in Southeast Asia in the late 1970s and 1980s said they frequently discovered that they were tracking heroin smugglers who were on the CIA payroll.[168]

One of those smugglers may have been Lu Hsu-shui, considered one of the top four heroin dealers in the entire Golden Triangle. He reportedly got his start in the business "trading opium for gold with KMT remnants in northern Thailand." The CIA shut down the DEA's investigation of him, claiming it had to use the drug agency's key informant "in a high-level, sensitive national security operation."[169]

In 1973, U.S. authorities arrested a Thai national, Puttaporn Khramkhruan, in connection with the seizure of 59 pounds of opium in Chicago. The CIA quashed the case, according to a Justice Department memorandum, lest it "prove embarrassing because of Mr. Khramkhruan's involvement with the CIA activities in Thailand, Burma and elsewhere." Khramkhruan, a former officer in the KMT's dope-smuggling army, served the Agency as an informant on narcotics trafficking in northern Thailand and claimed the CIA had full knowledge of his actions. When the story later leaked, Sen. Charles Percy commented, "Apparently CIA agents are untouchable—however serious their crime or however much harm is done to society. Last year [1974] we learned that the President of the United States himself is not above the law. Yet apparently CIA agents are untouchable."[170]

Perhaps the biggest fish of all to escape was Thai General Kriangsak Chamanand, who helped lead a particularly bloody military coup in 1976 and then took power himself in another coup in 1977. Kriangsak, a graduate of the National Defense University in the United States, had served as a "key link" in CIA covert operations during the Vietnam War, including the use of Thai mercenaries to fight the "secret war" in Laos.[171]

Publicly, American drug agents gave Kriangsak a clean bill of health. But author James Mills, who had access to DEA files, states:

> Kriangsak himself is named in classified intelligence reports (and by other sources as well) as the direct recipient of secret cash payoffs from leaders of armed groups controlling opium traffic in the mountains of Thailand and Burma... These groups include at least three [KMT] rebel armies with past or present clandestine

support of the American CIA.[172]

Southeast Asia is hardly the only theater where drug smugglers turned up as protected CIA "assets." In the early 1970s, the CIA immunized Latin American smugglers in no fewer than 27 federal drug cases. Such outcomes were not mere bad luck. A former DEA operations chief recalls that, starting with CIA directors William Colby and George Bush, the Agency regularly poached from both the DEA's pool of informants and investigative targets. "When the DEA arrested these drug traffickers," he stated, "they used the CIA as protection and because of their CIA involvement they were released. This amounted to a license to traffic for life because even if they were arrested in the future, they could demand classified documents about their prior CIA involvement and would have to be let go. The CIA knew full well that their assets were drug traffickers."[173]

THE MEXICAN CONNECTION

One of the most astonishingly successful entrepreneurs of modern times was Alberto Sicilia-Falcon, a Cuban-born narcotics trafficker who reached the pinnacle of his profession at the tender age of 31. When Mexican police arrested him in 1975, U.S. authorities termed him "the leader of the world's largest cocaine and marijuana trafficking organization." Sicilia modestly denied all the credit. He declared that his far-flung drug operations had been protected by the CIA, which allegedly had trained him in the early 1960s as a soldier in the secret war against Castro. The more DEA agents investigated his case, the less they could dismiss such claims as fantasy.[174]

But even Sicilia's operation paled in comparison to a much vaster narcotics syndicate blessed and protected by the CIA: the Direccion Federal de Seguridad (DFS), a powerful internal security agency sometimes compared to a joint CIA and FBI.

The DFS, in fact, protected and profited from Sicilia before his downfall. But his fate made no difference to officials of this agency. With so many other traffickers to choose from, he was expendable. In the crackdown on Mexican traffickers that followed the murder of DEA agent Enrique Camarena in 1985, U.S. investigators discovered that DFS agents handled security for many of Mexico's most notorious smugglers. "Every time we grab someone, they're carrying a card from the DFS," complained one drug agent.[175]

Later evidence suggested that the DFS was not merely a hired gun of the infamous "Guadalajara Cartel," which shipped more Colombian cocaine into the United States than any other syndicate. It actually masterminded that cartel's whole operation. According to one well-placed American informant, DFS settled a bloody feud between several of Mexico's leading drug families, relocated them to Guadalajara, provided them with bodyguards and local political protection, stamped out their competition and even provided the logistics for moving drugs into the United States. For these services, the DFS took a quarter of the cartel's profits.[176]

Mexican trafficker Carlos de Herrera called the DFS one of the "most strong mafias in Mexico." The agency, he testified, "had a ranch specially built just to grow marijuana..." When DEA agents led Mexican Federal Judicial Police (rivals of the DFS) to the ranch, they seized 10,000 tons of marijuana, worth more than $5 billion, and detained more than 5,000 field workers. It gave new meaning to the word agribusiness.[177]

The DFS, in turn, enjoyed the full backing of the CIA—despite American awareness by the early 1970s of its criminal operations. To protect the fruits of their relationship—access to Mexican intelligence on subversive movements and East bloc diplomatic activities—Washington turned a blind eye to the river of drugs the DFS sent north. Indeed, the CIA had DFS chief Miguel Nazar Haro on its payroll for a decade, the DEA learned. When Nazar was indicted in 1982 for running an enormous stolen car ring from the United States into Mexico, the CIA intervened to block his prosecution. It named him as the agency's "most important source in Mexico and Central America." An embassy officer cabled Washington, "CIA station and [FBI legal attache] believe our mutual interests and as a consequence the security of the United States, as it relates to terrorism, intelligence, and counterintelligence in Mexico, would suffer a disastrous blow if Nazar were forced to resign." When the U.S. attorney who brought the case objected publicly to this obstruction of justice, he was summarily fired.[178]

Nazar's successor as chief of DFS, Jose Antonio Zorrilla, was no less corrupt. He took vast amounts of money from the drug lords to protect their interests, all the while maintaining close contact with the CIA station in Mexico City. This relationship made the DFS untouchable. "They don't give a damn," said one DEA agent of the CIA. "They turn their heads the other way. They see their task as much more important than ours." The CIA "protected that agency for so long," complained retired DEA investigator James Kuykendall. "They didn't want their connection with the DFS to ever go away, and the DFS just got out of hand." The CIA refused to cooperate with DEA investigations that could have uncovered the role of this sinister security organization in forging one of the world's greatest drug syndicates.[179]

Only with Camarena's murder did the balance of forces shift enough for the CIA to begin adding drug enforcement to its agenda in Mexico. Testimony by government witnesses at the trials of Camarena's accused killers, however, has implicated the CIA in protecting some of Mexico's leading drug lords in return for their financial support of the Nicaraguan Contras.[180]

THE NICARAGUAN CONTRAS

Wherever the CIA engages in Third World paramilitary operations, there will almost surely be found an explosion in drug smuggling by local partisans—not only to finance the cause, but also to take advantage of the protection and secrecy afforded by the U.S. government in the name of "national security." The Nicaraguan Contras were no exception; what made their story unusual was the close attention paid to their drug involvement by some members of the media and by a Senate subcommittee under John Kerry of Massachusetts.

In April 1989—too long after the emotional high point of the Iran-Contra scandal to make any political difference—Kerry's subcommittee issued a 1,166 page report on drug corruption in Central America and the Caribbean, with particular attention to U.S. and Contra complicity in the cocaine trade.

Its conclusions were blockbusters, even if drowned out by the din of official drug-war rhetoric. "There was substantial evidence of drug smuggling through the war zones on the part of individual Contras, Contra suppliers, Contra pilots, mercenaries who worked with the Contras, and Contra supporters throughout the region," the subcommittee concluded.[181]

Far from taking steps to combat those crimes, "U.S. officials involved in Central America failed to address the drug issue for fear of jeopardizing the war efforts against Nicaragua," the subcommittee showed. "In each case," its report added, "one or another agency of the U.S. government had information regarding the involvement either while it was occurring, or immediately thereafter." Even worse, "senior U.S. policy makers were not immune to the idea that drug money was a perfect solution to the Contras' funding problems.[182]

Reagan administration officials did their best to frustrate, stonewall and derail the investigation. But even some of the most partisan defenders of the Contra cause had to admit a problem. The head of the CIA's Central America Task Force confessed during congressional hearings in 1987, "With respect to (drug trafficking by) the Resistance Forces…it is not a couple of people. It is a lot of people."[183]

Knowledge of that troubling fact did nothing to stop U.S. aid from flowing directly to criminal sectors of the Nicaraguan resistance. The Kerry subcommittee discovered that State Department contracts worth $806,000 went to no fewer than four aid conduits "owned and operated by narcotics traffickers."[184]

One of these was SETCO Air, a Honduran cargo firm hired by the State Department to transport goods to the Contras in 1985 and 1986. As early as 1983, a Customs report identified the firm as a front for "Juan Ramon Matta Ballesteros, a Class I DEA violator." Matta was no ordinary smuggler. A billionaire, he ranked until his arrest in 1988 as one of the biggest traffickers of all time. As one DEA spokesman declared in 1989, "He is the kind of individual who would be a decision-maker of last resort. He is at the same level as the rulers of the Medellin and Cali cartels." Matta made his fortune by connecting the Colombian cocaine producers with the CIA-DFS-protected Guadalajara Cartel in Mexico.[185]

The Reagan administration's de facto protection of Matta, a result of its Contra policy, represented a much bigger blow to the war on drugs than the smuggling operations of any particular resistance group. Matta practically owned Honduras, where he corrupted the same ruling military officers whom the CIA relied on to provide sanctuary and support for the Contras. For the CIA, that conflict of interest—between running an efficient guerrilla war and fighting drugs—was no real conflict at all. The CIA blocked a proposal by DEA agents to open a grand jury investigation of drug corruption within the Honduran military.[186] Shortly thereafter, in mid-1983, the DEA actually shut down its office in Tegucigalpa and moved out of the country.

As one former high-level American diplomat in the region explained, "Without the support of the Honduran military, there would have been no such thing as the Contras. It's that simple. If evidence were developed linking the Honduran military to cocaine trafficking, the administration would have to take action—causing an immediate and conclusive end to the Contras—or purposely turn a blind eye to what was going on. Neither alternative was particularly appealing. So they got rid of [the DEA station] before they were forced into taking a serious look in the first place."[187]

The result could have been predicted: Honduras became a booming center for multi-ton loads of Colombian cocaine. One such shipment in 1987, totaling more than four tons, produced the largest seizure of cocaine in U.S. history to that time. The DEA itself estimated that "only" a fifth of all U.S. cocaine moved through Honduras; other estimates put the figure as high as one-half. But when the chief investigator for the House Subcommittee on Crime ventured to check out the situation, the U.S. embassy in Tegucigalpa blocked his probe.[188]

Matta, wanted in the United States for the murder of DEA agent Camarena, continued to live a charmed life, entertaining high-level officials and directing a far-flung criminal network from his lavish mansion in Tegucigalpa. Only in 1988—after the Contra cause was moribund—did U.S. drug agents finally force his extradition from Honduras, and then only by promising immunity to the corrupt military officers who harbored him.[189]

THE CIA'S MAN IN PANAMA

Closely interwoven with the Contra story—and ultimately much more embarrassing for officials of the Reagan-Bush administration—is the case of Gen. Manuel Noriega. The Panamanian strongman received Washington's financial and diplomatic support for a good fifteen years after the first clear indications of his drug crimes began showing up in intelligence files.

First recruited as an agent by the U.S. Defense Intelligence Agency in 1959, Noriega went on the CIA's payroll in 1967. After a military coup in

1968, Noriega took charge of Panama's intelligence service, making him all the more invaluable to the Agency. He passed along inside information, provided services for covert operations and facilitated the use of Panama as a major center of U.S. intelligence gathering in Latin America.

In 1976, CIA Director George Bush paid Noriega $110,000 a year for these services and put the Panamanian up as a house guest of his deputy director. Payments to Noriega, suspended in the Carter years, resumed in 1981 when President Reagan took office. At their peak, in 1985, Noriega collected $200,000 from the CIA.[190]

That raise reflected Noriega's key role in supporting the Reagan administration's "covert" war against the Nicaraguan Sandinistas. In the early days of that operation, Noriega supplied pilots who helped smuggle weapons to the Contras. In 1984, he contributed $100,000 to Contra forces based in Costa Rica. In 1985, according to one of Noriega's former aides, he promised to help train Contra units and let them use Panama as a transit point. Noriega also helped Oliver North, the National Security Council aide who oversaw the Contra operation, plan and carry out a major sabotage raid in Managua. The two men met in September 1986, shortly before the Iran-Contra scandal broke, to discuss further sabotage against Nicaraguan economic targets, including an oil refinery and airport.[191]

In January 1988, after Noriega's usefulness to the Contra cause had ended, the Reagan administration approved his indictment on drug charges. By then, the Kerry subcommittee noted, "the United States had received substantial information about the criminal involvement of top Panamanian officials for nearly twenty years and done little to respond."[192]

Indeed, as early as 1971 the BNDD prepared enough evidence against Noriega in a major marijuana smuggling case to indict—only to be turned down by the U.S. attorney's office in Miami for practical reasons: No one in those days imagined invading Panama to bring him to justice. Federal drug agents did, however, consider assassinating him or leaking disinformation to connect him to a plot against his superior, Gen. Omar Torrijos. Instead, BNDD chose to coöperate rather than fight, a pattern that lasted through several administrations in Washington.[193]

The CIA, in particular, helped see to it that no political harm came to

Noriega until he became a public liability. Author James Mills recounted in 1986 that "When the DEA boss in Panama City suggested an SFIP- (Special Field Intelligence Program) to unravel the shadowy background of billions of dollars of Panama-stashed drug money, he sought necessary approval from the CIA station chief. The station chief agreed, but with an interesting reservation. If the SFIP developed any information involving Panamanian government officials, that particular aspect of the investigation must be immediately dropped." CIA Director William Casey was the Reagan administration's staunchest defender of Noriega. Even after Casey's death, the Agency refused to make available its file on Noriega to the DEA or the U.S. attorney who brought the indictment against him.[194]

Now that the U.S.-backed opposition is in charge, it remains to be seen whether anything will really change. President Guillermo Endara has refused to consider any significant changes in Panama's notorious bank secrecy laws, which have made the country a haven for flight capital and drug money. He is a protegé of corrupt former President Arnulfo Arias and director of Banco Interoceanico, an institution implicated in laundering drug money. Endara's attorney general, treasury minister and supreme court chief justice—three rather critical officials—were all directors of the First Interamericas Bank, owned and operated by the heads of Colombia's powerful Cali cocaine cartel. These and other similar appointments do not seem to trouble Washington as long as the new regime's retains its pro-American stance.[195]

AFGHANISTAN: HOLY WARRIORS AND HEROIN

Drug smuggling facilitated by CIA allies in Central America supplied a large fraction of all the cocaine that reached the United States in the mid-1980s. In exactly the same period—but with none of the publicity— CIA allies in Afghanistan and Pakistan opened an even larger drug pipeline into the U.S. market. In the process, they gave an enormous boost to their trafficking intermediaries: powerful Sicilian crime syndicates now entrenched in the United States and numerous other countries around the world.[196]

Jack Blum, who investigated the Contra connection for the Kerry subcommittee, calls the Afghanistan drug scandal "one of the biggest uncovered stories in the foreign policy arena. The scale and duration of the connection between drug trafficking, gun running and foreign policy are far larger even than the Central American affair." The numbers bear him out. While the CIA was shipping more than a billion dollars worth of arms into Afghanistan, the guerrillas it backed helped to boost the country's opium production from 250 tons in 1982 to about 800 tons in 1989. The region supplied most of the heroin for the infamous "Pizza Connection," a Sicilian Mafia network partially busted (with great fanfare) by the DEA in 1984. By 1985, as much as 62 percent of all American heroin came from Afghanistan and Pakistan.[197]

The CIA didn't introduce opium to Afghanistan, nor was it the first to grasp the political implications of widespread cultivation. By the early 1970s, American experts had evidence that at least some of the trade was controlled or protected by members of the court and royal family of King Mohammed Zahir Shah.[198]

Official support for the drug trade ended only after April 1978, when Nur Mohammed Taraki took power in a Marxist coup. One of his first measures, undertaken with help from United Nations experts, was to break up the country's large feudal estates and suppress the cultivation of opium on them. The Taraki government's harsh reforms—including its vigorous anti-narcotics campaign—triggered the beginning of a revolt by semi-autonomous tribal groups that traditionally raised opium for export. The Kabul regime in turn stepped up its "war on drugs" in order to deny revenue to the rebel Mujahedeen, who began expanding production to finance their insurgency.[199]

As early as the spring of 1979, before Washington committed to the rebels, press accounts revealed their financial dependence on drugs. U.S. narcotics experts reported in 1980 that Afghan guerrillas were fighting "on a schedule determined in part by opium poppy planting and harvest seasons." The DEA predicted, quite rightly, that Afghanistan and its neighbors "could become pre-eminent in the U.S. and Western European market in the 1980s."[200]

But drug enforcement took second place to international geopolitics. The Carter administration interpreted the Soviet invasion as a wholesale break with detente along the "arc of crisis" stretching from Angola through Ethiopia and South Yemen to Southwest Asia. Busy organizing support from Saudi Arabia and the People's Republic of China to contain Soviet aggression, the White House ranked drugs low on its list of priorities.

At the same time, it was aware of the potential for embarrassment. One "high level" law enforcement official in Washington told Hoag Levins of *Philadelphia Magazine* in 1980, "You have the administration tiptoeing around this like it's a land mine. The issue of opium and heroin in Afghanistan is explosive... In the State of the Union speech, the president mentioned drug abuse but he was very careful to avoid mentioning Afghanistan, even though Afghanistan is where things are *really* happening right now... Why aren't we taking a more critical look at the arms we are now shipping in to gangs of drug runners who are obviously going to use them to increase the efficiency of their drug smuggling operation?"[201]

That same year, two members of President Carter's White House Strategy Council on Drug Abuse went public with an extraordinary column in the *New York Times*. "Our requests for information that by law we are entitled to receive have been met in some instances by delays of years, at other times with only superficial responses," they complained. "...For example, we worry about the growing of opium poppies in Afghanistan and Pakistan by rebel tribesmen who apparently are the chief adversaries of the Soviet troops in Afghanistan. Are we erring in befriending these tribes as we did in Laos when Air America (chartered by the Central Intelligence Agency) helped transport crude opium from certain tribal areas?"[202]

One of the co-authors recalled ten years later: "There was a wall of silence. We got not a single response to the article."[203]

Afghan rebel involvement in the heroin trade became the great "unmentionable" in Washington. Worthy though the cause of resisting Soviet aggression was, it might be a harder sell if the public knew who their tax dollars were supporting. By keeping the support program "covert" through CIA channels, no one had to discuss the tradeoffs. The White House didn't talk, Congress didn't ask and the media never really investigated.

Indicative of this official silence was the absence of any section on Afghanistan in the State Department's annual narcotics report for 1985. In the 1986 edition, all of a sudden, the department acknowledged that Afghanistan was "probably the world's largest producer of opium for export" and "the poppy source for a majority of the Southwest Asian heroin found in the United States and 80 percent of the heroin and morphine in Europe." As to possible rebel involvement in the traffic, however, it stated only: "The Mujahideen organizations have condemned opium production and use."[204]

Glimmers of truth occasionally poked through the blackout. "You can say the rebels make their money off the sale of opium," admitted David Melocik, the DEA's congressional liaison, in 1983. "There's no doubt about it. The rebels keep their cause going through the sale of opium." Melocik indicated that no less than half of all U.S. heroin came "from that area" of the world—making American support for the Mujahedeen, in his candid words, a "double-edged sword."[205]

Government authorities declined, however, to say who the ultimate producers were. Ambassador Deane Hinton, who oversaw U.S. covert aid to the rebels, told a congressional study mission that "no hard evidence exists of Afghan freedom fighters exchanging opium for arms"—the same sort of hedged denial heard for years about Panama's Gen. Manuel Noriega. Hinton thus preserved the fig leaf needed to maintain the arms aid program intact.[206]

A few intrepid reporters and academics broke through the wall of silence and deception late in the game to name some of the top rebel commanders implicated in the opium and heroin trade.

Perhaps the most notorious of them, Gulbuddin Hekmatyar, may accurately be described as an assassin and terrorist. Responsible for murdering hundreds of dedicated resistance fighters, political workers and intellectuals who refused his demands for supreme leadership of the movement, Gulbuddin even made alliances with Communist forces in Kabul to advance himself and his Islamic Party. It was entirely within character, therefore, that he reportedly emerged as a leading figure in the heroin trade, using his longstanding Pakistani military connections to arrange protection and transportation. (Another party of the same name, led by Gulbuddin's fundamentalist rival Younis Khalis, reportedly also owns heroin laboratories in the border town of Ribat al Ali.)

Gulbuddin fought a two-year war with another powerful rebel commander, Nasim Akhundzada, for control of the rich poppy fields of Helmand, a province on Afghanistan's southern border with Pakistan. Nasim, a cruel warlord, became deputy defense minister of the Afghan

Interim Government after the Soviet withdrawal. His awesome opium farms, stretching colorfully for miles, were watered by a pre-war irrigation project built at U.S. taxpayers' expense to make the Helmand Valley the bread basket of Afghanistan. In 1989, Nasim entered into negotiations with Robert Oakley, the American ambassador in Pakistan, to curb opium production in return for millions of dollars in aid payments. Washington reportedly turned him down, but continued to finance and arm him indirectly through his Islamic Revolutionary Movement. Nasim succeeded in holding off not only Gulbuddin but Mohammed Yahya of the Islamic Union for the Liberation of Afghanistan, who fought a bloody battle in September 1989 for control of a strategic opium shipment route. In March 1990, however, Nasim's luck ran out. Assassins gunned down the rebel opium lord and six bodyguards near the Pakistani city of Peshawar, gateway to eastern Afghanistan. Many experts point to Gulbuddin as the likely culprit.[207]

Explaining why Washington chose not to confront these unsavory Afghan allies or their Pakistani patrons for flooding the world with heroin, one U.S. official told the *Washington Post*, "You can't look at [drugs] in a vacuum separated from the overall policy."[208]

The official silence did not only serve to maintain public support for the Mujahedeen cause. It also smoothed relations with the regime of General Mohammed Zia Ul-Haq in Pakistan, which channeled CIA support to the rebels across the border.

The Zia regime was, in fact, thoroughly corrupt. Opium grown in Afghanistan was (and still is) shipped out and refined in Pakistan under the watchful eye of powerful Pakistani commanders, the military intelligence service ISI, and the army's National Logistics Cell, which trucks goods between Karachi and Afghan refugee camps on the border free from the prying eyes of narcotics police. Close associates of President Zia reportedly implicated in the heroin trade included his chief minister, personal banker, personal pilot and daughter's physician. Pakistani sources estimate the value of the trade at $8 billion a year, almost double the country's annual budget.[209]

Details of this corruption emerged from official U.S. sources only after it the Soviets began pulling out of Afghanistan—and after Washington had grown disenchanted with ISI's manipulation of U.S. aid to support fundamentalist, anti-Western rebel leaders like Gulbuddin.

In 1988, the General Accounting Office acknowledged that "Pakistan has a corruption problem" and cited the complaint of U.S. officials that "not a single significant Pakistani trafficker" had been imprisoned before 1984. Subsequent arrests, those officials added, were for show and the culprits were usually "quietly released after serving only a few months." By 1989, Pakistan had no fewer than 100 heroin labs near the border with Afghanistan.[210]

Why didn't the DEA, at least, make a public fuss? One possible reason, according to the *Financial Times*, may be that "The 17 U.S. drug enforcement officers in Islamabad include some from the CIA who work closely with the ISI on the Afghan war and are thus aligned to the very men involved." That was also the opinion of one Pathan opium lord who noted the "symbiotic relationship" between the CIA, Pakistani military intelligence and his own business. "It's funny that the CIA are using the very people the State Department are trying to stop," he told a reporter.[211]

Washington had reasons other than regional politics to keep silent. A full investigation might produce embarrassing revelations of shady CIA money laundering operations. In the spring of 1989, *Newsweek* revealed that the CIA had used an obscure Lebanese-controlled currency firm in Zurich, Shakarchi Trading, to channel aid to the Afghan rebels. The DEA investigated the same firm for "mingling the currency of heroin, morphine base, hashish traffickers with that of jewelers buying gold on the black market and Middle East arms traffickers." Shakarchi was implicated in huge money laundering operations for leaders of the Turkish mafia, including the organization of Yasar Musullulu, whose eight-ton shipment of morphine base from Afghanistan amply supplied the Sicilian "Pizza Connection" in the United States in the early 1980s. Shakarchi has also been named as a repository of funds from the Iran-Contra arms trio, Richard Secord, Albert Hakim, and their Geneva financial wizard, Willard Zucker.[212]

By 1989, however, with the Soviet withdrawal achieved, Washington felt freer to register its unhappiness with the drug situation through a semi-official leak to the *New York Times*:

> The United States has asked the Afghan rebel government in exile to curb the soaring production of opium poppies in areas of Afghanistan that its guerrillas control, administration officials said

today. Robert B. Oakley, the American Ambassador to Pakistan, expressed concern about the cultivation and trafficking in opium during a meeting in Islamabad about a week ago with Sibghatullah Mojadedi, the president of the government in exile, and Abdul Rasul Sayaf, its prime minister... A State Department official said, 'We are beginning to put the rebels on notice that drug trafficking could damage their prospects for a high level of American assistance in their reconstruction efforts.' ...Afghanistan is the second-largest producer of opium in the world... An estimated 87 percent of all opium is grown in Nangarhar province and in the Helmand valley, most of which are in the hands of the rebels... It is an open secret that some rebel commanders have used opium profits to help finance their operations against the Soviet-backed Government of Afghanistan in Kabul. American intelligence officials acknowledge that individual rebels and even small units serve as drug couriers. These officials said they have long suspected that planes, trucks and mules ferrying American military equipment into Afghanistan are also used to ship drugs to Pakistan. Over the years the United States has done little to press the Afghan rebels to curb the drug trade.[213]

By 1990, administration officials no longer relied on leaks; they went public with their concerns. Melvyn Levitsky, the State Department's top narcotics officer, told a press conference in Islamabad:

What we have made very clear to the Mujhahedeen commanders is that they must stay out of drugs and that they must discourage production of drugs. We cannot accept a situation where we are giving assistance to the Mujahedeen and they on the other hand are encouraging drug production and drug trafficking... The point we have made to the Mujahedeen is that if there is considerable evidence that there is...support for drug production and drug trafficking we would not be able to assist that government.[214]

Even with so public an admission by a prominent U.S. official of the complicity of Washington's allies in the heroin trade, the American media and Congress have hardly taken notice. The "war on drugs," it seems, inspires much passion but little debate. "After all the years I put into the public sector," commented former Kerry subcommittee chief counsel Jack Blum, "I am sick to death of the truths that cannot be spoken."[215]

DRUGS AND COVERT INTELLIGENCE NETWORKS

At least two factors seem to have fostered the CIA's close, even collusive relationship with so many international traffickers. One of the Agency's responsibilities is to keep tabs on underworld networks whose financial resources, expertise in secret operations and access to corruptible government officials make them a significant political force. As one leading State Department official noted in 1985, drug profits "can buy an election, finance a supply of arms for insurgency and, in sum, destabilize legitimate governments and subordinate democratic processes."[216]

Anyone who can buy an election or destabilize a government is a potentially valuable asset as well as a legitimate intelligence target. Criminal syndicates, usually hostile to Communism, made logical Cold War allies: They could provide conduits for money laundering, "deniable" agents for covert operations, and valuable intelligence on the dirty underside of foreign politics. "The fact is," remarked Gen. Paul F. Gorman, former head of the U.S. Southern Command, "if you want to go into the subversion business, collect intelligence and move arms, you deal with the drug movers."[217]

Consider one such informal network of CIA assets and drug-related operatives associated with the late Florida attorney Paul Helliwell. As head of OSS wartime intelligence in China, he dealt with the notorious Chinese secret police chief and narcotics smuggler Tai Li. Helliwell reportedly also made a regular practice of buying information from tribesmen in the China-Burma-India theater with five-pound bars of opium. Returning to civilian life in Florida, he continued to work for the CIA. In 1951 he helped set up Sea Supply Corp., a front used to run supplies to the KMT troops stranded in northeastern Burma after the Chinese revolution; it also ran the KMT's opium out of the hill country to Bangkok. Later Helliwell laundered CIA funds through the Bahamas-based Castle Bank.[218]

Castle Bank catered to the tax-evasion set—notably several leading American gangsters with interests in Las Vegas. But it also did mysterious transactions with a Cayman Islands firm, ID Corp. ID's sole owner, the American Shig Katayama, became known as one of the key facilitators of Lockheed Corp.'s huge payoffs to Japanese politicians in return for airplane contracts. Of Katayama one Japanese journalist charged, "his real job (in the early 1950s) was to handle narcotics for the U.S. intelligence work."[219]

Lockheed disbursed money to the politicians through the rightist "wire-puller" Yoshio Kodama, who enjoyed unsurpassed influence in the ruling Liberal Democratic Party. During World War II Kodama proved himself a gifted smuggler and procurement specialist for the Japanese navy, on whose behalf he traded opium and heroin for scarce raw materials. Arrested after VJ-day as a class-A war criminal suspect, Kodama was released from prison in 1948 and quickly recruited by the CIA, which used him, among other purposes, when it needed leverage over politicians in Tokyo. Investigators of the corporate bribes trail have concluded that the CIA "orchestrated much of Lockheed's financial operations in Japan pursuant to covert US foreign policy objectives... particularly in support of ultraconservative groups."[220]

Lending weight to that deduction was the role of another intermediary in the bribery conduit, the international currency dealer Deak & Co. Founded by OSS veteran Nicholas Deak, it was reportedly used by the CIA to finance covert operations, including the 1953 overthrow of Iranian Prime Minister Mohammed Mossadeq.[221]

Deak & Co. was also said to be the channel by which the CIA's Saigon station traded millions of dollars on the black market to supplement its appropriation—at the expense of American taxpayers who propped up Vietnam's currency. The firm also moved money for at least one notorious underworld figure who also played the black market in Saigon. He in turn was visited in 1968 by a powerful American Mafia boss (and veteran of CIA plots to assassinate Fidel Castro), who apparently was looking for new sources of heroin following the disruption of traditional European suppliers. No wonder Deak & Co. was called the "Black Bank of Asia."[222]

Finally, the Deak firm came under fire in 1984 by the President's Commission on Organized Crime, which accused it of laundering millions of dollars (perhaps unwittingly) on behalf of Colombian cocaine traffickers.[223]

One Deak employee who allegedly boasted of playing a role in the transfer of Lockheed bribe funds to top Japanese officials, Ron Pulger-Frame, also carried money for the Nugan Hand Bank of Australia, whose principals specialized in moving drugs, hot money, and arms around the world. Its network included prominent CIA veterans, U.S. military intelligence and special operations experts, and members of the Australian underworld. Reporter Jonathan Kwitny suggests that Nugan Hand might have been "expanded under an arrangement with the CIA to replace [its] failing Caribbean front banks"—including Castle Bank—in the late 1970s. A decade later, several American covert operations veterans in Nugan Hand's milieu, including Richard Secord and Thomas Clines, would become implicated in the Iran-Contra scandal.[224]

NARCOTICS AGENTS, CIA AGENTS

If intelligence and drug trafficking have often been intertwined, so have intelligence and drug enforcement—or at least the pretense of drug enforcement. From the days of the Federal Bureau of Narcotics to the DEA, the CIA has taken cover in anti-drug agencies even as its intrigues undercut their law enforcement ends.

The police training and assistance programs taken over from the Office of Public Safety by DEA and the State Department's narcotics section, for example, functioned as CIA fronts from their inception. The longtime head of OPS was former CIA counterintelligence specialist Byron Engle. The CIA used OPS to supply credentials to its overseas agents and simplify liaison with local police who supplied intelligence on dissident politics and personalities. The CIA was also happy to further the OPS's counterinsurgency mission—even to the point of assigning Green Beret instructors to teach foreign police students how to build and set off bombs.[225]

The CIA used its opium-and-arms smuggling front Sea Supply Corp., among other things, to train the paramilitary Thai Border Patrol Police under Gen. Phao Sriyanon. The CIA aimed to mould the BPP into a counterinsurgency asset beholden to Washington rather than the Thai government. CIA assistance enabled Phao "to build the police force into a powerful military organization which was better led, better paid and more efficient than the army," according to one former CIA analyst. Before long, Thailand had "one of the highest ratios between policemen and citizens of any country in the world."[226]

But Phao was also the most notorious Thai drug smuggler of his era. The contacts he established through the CIA's Sea Supply Corp. with the KMT opium traffickers allowed him to sew up a near-monopoly on

Burmese opium exports. His border police escorted drug caravans from the frontier through to Bangkok.[227]

A 1957 coup unseated Phao, but the CIA continued to aid the BPP under OPS cover. In the early 1970s, as noted above, a CIA employee in this program was caught smuggling a load of opium into the United States. The Justice Department dropped charges in order to protect the operation's cover.[228]

That embarrassment didn't prevent U.S. narcotics aid from flowing to the BPP to make up for the loss of the OPS program in 1974. The political fruits of that aid ripened in the bloody military coup of October 6, 1976—led in part by Gen. Kriangsak, protector of the KMT drug lords. BPP units, backed by OPS-trained and INC-supplied elements of the Bangkok police, burst into Thammasat University to crush student demonstrators. "Their revenge [against the students] was taken in meting out humiliations, in mutilations brutally inflicted, in burning a student alive and in simple wholesale murder," according to one academic account of the coup. "Thousands of unarmed students were killed, injured or arrested, and a few days later, most of the liberal to left journalists, scholars and intellectuals were also rounded up and put in prison or 'rehabilitation camps.'" *The Washington Post* observed, in an editorial, "Surprisingly, or perhaps not so surprisingly, no one in the Ford administration has been heard to utter a single public word of regret for the demise of Thai democracy." Indeed, within days the United States rewarded the new regime by giving the BPP five helicopters—supposedly to fight drugs.[229]

U.S. intelligence reports indicated several years later that the Border Patrol Police were still protecting leading traffickers and using official vehicles to transport heroin south to Bangkok. No less an authority than the KMT opium warlord Tuan Shi-wen branded them "totally corrupt and responsible for the transportation of narcotics." DEA agents, who considered the BPP still to be "a wholly owned subsidiary of the CIA," could only despair at the futility of their job. They had every reason to despair further in 1987, when the Pentagon pretended to do its part in the war on drugs by dispatching a Special Forces team to train the BPP in what could only have been counterinsurgency tactics.[230]

The CIA's undercover use of narcotics agencies and programs did not become a significant public issue until 1975, when the Rockefeller

Commission revealed that the CIA had infiltrated agents into the BNDD on an improper domestic counterintelligence mission.[231] Long before, however, Harry Anslinger had permitted his narcotics bureau agents to assist in foreign covert operations. As when he falsely denounced Red China as the source of America's narcotics plague, Anslinger subverted law enforcement to serve the ends of the CIA and Cold War politics.

Anslinger himself got his start in the field during World War I, working with the State Department's privately funded Bureau of Secret Intelligence. Rising in 1930 to become the first director of the Federal Bureau of Narcotics, he maintained a lively interest in foreign political intelligence as part of his job.[232]

Garland Williams, head of the FBN's New York office and the first agent ever sent overseas by the bureau, became chief of the Army's Counter-Intelligence Corps in 1940 and then Director of Special Training for the OSS, where he taught hundreds of agents in the arts of "espionage, sabotage and guerrilla tactics." (According to Anslinger, "many agents" followed Williams' lead in joining the OSS.) He also served as liaison to the British Special Operations Executive, famed for its covert operations during the World War II. In the Korean War he commanded a military intelligence group. In the early 1960s, several years after retiring from the FBN, he helped several African nations set up police and intelligence services—a job he could hardly have undertaken without CIA approval.[233]

After the war, FBN agents collaborated with OSS's successor. One, Hank Manfredi, doubled as a CIA agent in Rome. The Agency considered his "contribution to the attainment of the U.S. Government objectives" to be "oustanding." Another agent, Sal Vizzini, took on a special undercover assignment for the agency in Beirut. "As a narcotics agent I'd have a certain immunity from government surveillance," he explained. "I'd have a cover within a cover, which was more than you could say for the CIA regulars on the scene." Vizzini also worked with the CIA station in Bangkok in the early 1960s in a plot to bomb a major KMT heroin manufacturer in Burma.[234]

George White, one of Anslinger's top men, also had a cover-within-a-cover. A lieutenant colonel in OSS, he rose to direct all counterintelligence training. Because of what the CIA called his "good access to criminal types," the agency recruited him in 1952 to set up apartments where secret drug tests could be conducted on unwitting subjects. The tests related to interrogation, "mind control," and disabling of human targets. Helping White to set them up was another narcotics agent and OSS veteran, Charles Siragusa.

"The particular advantage of these arrangements with the Bureau of Narcotics officials has been that test subjects could be sought and cultivated within the setting of narcotics control," the CIA explained in one memo. "Some subjects have been informers or members of suspect criminal elements from whom the bureau has obtained results of operational value through the tests."[235]

The CIA's drug tests, according to another memo, were meant to "develop means for the control of the activities and mental capacities of individuals whether willing or not." Operation ARTICHOKE, in particular, asked whether an individual could "be made to perform an act of attempted assassination, involuntarily" and suggested testing possible methods "against a prominent (deleted) politician or if necessary against an American official..." After the Manchurian Candidate did his job, the CIA assumed he would be "taken into custody...and 'disposed of.' "[236]

The CIA justified such distasteful programs with the claim, advanced by its fabled counterintelligence chief James Angleton, that the Soviets and Chinese were developing similar drugs. Angleton had been George White's wartime colleague in OSS counterintelligence; the two remained close colleagues in the postwar years and met frequently as the CIA's drug testing program got underway.[237]

The CIA officer responsible for this tightly held program also recruited Mafia drug traffickers for the murder plots against Fidel Castro in 1960.[238]

The FBN was no stranger to those plots, either. In the summer of 1960 a CIA officer approached Charles Siragusa, by then deputy director of the FBN and official liaison with the CIA, with the news that the agency was forming an "assassination squad." "Since you have a lot of contacts with the underworld," he told Siragusa, "we'd like you to put together a team to conduct a series of hits... There's some foreign leaders we'd like dead."[239]

The FBN official declined—it was peacetime, after all—but the CIA found another back channel for its purpose.

The CIA recruited potential assassins though a reliable intermediary, known by his code-name QJ/WIN. A European criminal hired first to help kill Patrice Lumumba in the Congo, QJ/WIN had first been contacted "in connection with an illegal narcotics operation into the United States" and "in behalf of the Bureau of Narcotics." That QJ/WIN was in fact an important cog in the Corsican "French connection" is suggested by the notes of a CIA conspirator who specified *"No American citizens or American residents for direct action. Corsicans recommended. Sicilians could leak to Mafia."*[240]

For advice on the Corsican underworld and narcotics, the CIA could turn to its in-house expert, Lucien Conein. The French-born covert operator had worked with the Corsicans during World War II as an OSS agent in France and Indochina (with Paul Helliwell), and later in Vietnam where he became the CIA's liaison with the generals who murdered President Ngo Dinh Diem in 1963. U.S. Senate investigators heard unconfirmed allegations—reminscent of Helliwell's methods in World War II—that Conein paid off friendly Vietnamese hill tribesmen with drugs they later sold to American troops.[241]

In 1971 Conein hired on with his CIA-buddy and Castro assassination plotter E. Howard Hunt to help the Nixon White House with political dirty tricks. After the Watergate break-in made Hunt's operation too hot to handle, the White House disposed of Conein by finding him a consulting job with the BNDD.[242]

Conein recruited to his staff a number of former CIA agents to undertake what he called "clandestine operations." That was a euphemism for something much bigger. "When you get down to it," one of his colleagues explained, "Conein was organizing an assassination program. He was frustrated by the big-time operators who were just too insulated to get to... He felt we couldn't win, the way things were going."[243]

Official reports of this project, first codenamed BUNCIN and later DEACON, indicate that its object was to create "an international network of deep cover assets" to "immobilize or eliminate international sources of illicit drugs and significant narcotic traffickers." All its recruits were "former Central Intelligence Agency assets who operated in the Miami area during the 1960s." Cover was so tight that "if necessary" the operation could "be 'blamed' on other governmental agencies, or even on the intelligence services of other nations." Although ostensibly aimed at drug traffickers, the intelligence gathered by DEACON included reports on "violation of neutrality laws, extremist groups and terrorism, and information of a political nature" as well as material "of an internal security nature." This political orientation may explain why, in the three-year existence of the project, DEACON produced only a single drug bust.[244]

In direct connection with DEACON, Conein in 1974 went shopping for assassination equipment from a firm connected with his OSS colleague Mitchel WerBell III. A Georgia-based arms dealer who did business with alleged drug financier Robert Vesco, WerBell was later indicted (and acquitted) on drug smuggling charges. "He would never get involved in a conspiracy to import marijuana," his attorney protested. "Guns, revolutions, maybe even assassinations, but he's not being tried on that." The attorney said WerBell had worked with a secret anti-drug unit directed out of the White House and had assisted Conein in "putting together assassination devices for the DEA."[245]

Conein could hardly be considered a lone wolf within the bureaucracy. On May 27, 1971, President Nixon ordered that $100 million be secretly budgeted for clandestine BNDD assassinations. Officials of the narcotics agency began talking of the need to establish "hit squads" and of aiming to disrupt the heroin trade with "150 key assassinations." The CIA, apparently, was willing to assist.[246]

The plots reached deep within the White House itself, which organized a secret unit under Howard Hunt and Gordan Liddy with the ostensible mission of prosecuting the administration's "war on drugs." Hunt, the CIA veteran-turned-"Plumber" who employed Conein in 1971, recruited CIA-trained Cuban exiles in late 1971 and the spring of 1972 to "waste" Panamanian leader Gen. Omar Torrijos. Though the strongman's alleged protection of heroin traffickers supplied the rationale, Torrijos was almost certainly targeted because of his independent, leftist political stance and his opposition to the administration's demand for a new 50-year lease on the Panama Canal. Hunt saw it as a chance "to knock off a Communist drug dealer." Perhaps only the abortive Watergate break-in, mounted by the Hunt-Liddy team, prevented the plot from coming to fruition.[247]

Assassinations may yet reemerge as a tool of covert drug policy. In

1989, Senator Joseph Lieberman of Connecticut called for reconsideration of "Executive Order 12333, which prohibits ordering the killing of foreign enemies in all circumstances... We have to begin to treat the [Colombian drug] cartel not just as a law enforcement target, but as another terrorist organization, as an organization with which we are involved in a war."[248]

The legal tools are now in place to implement his suggestion. A directive signed by President Reagan defined drug trafficking as a "national security" threat akin to terrorism. (Indeed, "narcoterrorism" is a term favored by drug warriors.) Both the CIA and Army now officially assert the legal authority to kill individuals designated by the president as "terrorists" who "pose an immediate threat to United States citizens or the national security of the United States." And military special operations forces, assigned to the front lines of the "war on drugs" in Latin America, are on the scene if needed to exercise that option. One government critic described their modus operandi: "They call themselves 'door knockers.' They knock on the door, and then go in and kill all the bad guys... And they don't think civilians can tell them anything. It's scary. You're talking about giving them carte blanche to do anything they want, anywhere they want, without answering to anyone."[249]

Chapter V

Conclusion

If you put aircraft carriers, jets, balloons, all around South America, if you link DEA agents arm in arm across the Mexican border, you're not going to stop one iota of drugs... We've got to demilitarize this drug war very quickly before we get into a real shooting war under the banner of a drug war.
— Former senior DEA agent Michael Levine[250]

Talk of resorting to assassinations to solve the drug problem reflects the extent of official desperation: No amount of spending on law enforcement seems to put a dent in world drug production or smuggling.

In early 1990, the State Department revised its estimates of world cocaine production up 94 percent, marijuana production up 270 percent and opium production up 53 percent. Even the Colombian government's unprecedented crackdown on the Medellin Cartel starting in the summer of 1989 merely pushed the traffickers temporarily to safer havens in Peru, Ecuador and above all, Brazil, where the potential for drug cultivation and smuggling is virtually unlimited.[251]

Cocaine, once the luxury drug of wealthy Americans, has become cheap enough to plague the poorest of inner cities. Drug supplies rose about as fast as spending on federal drug enforcement during the last decade. The wholesale price of cocaine fell by half (or more) between 1982 and 1988. In the same period, purity rose from about 12.5 percent to 70 percent. The modest tightening of supply in 1990 is unlikely to last, given the opening of new refineries in Peru and Bolivia.[252]

Any number of drug experts admit the hopelessness of the task. An 18-month study by the RAND Corporation concluded that "the most basic point is that the supply of drugs can never be eliminated." Attorney General William French Smith reluctantly confessed that "unless you can eliminate the demand for drugs, the amount of money is so large that the dealers will continue to take whatever risk is necessary." Michael Skol, deputy assistant secretary of state for inter-American affairs, declared in 1989: "The good news is that we have had a lot of success. The bad news is that it doesn't make any difference. We and the countries of the Andes could seize a hell of a lot more cocaine hydrochloride and would still be ineffective in preventing the drugs from reaching the streets of New York." "If the cartel in Colombia is shut down," admitted DEA Administrator John Lawn, "other cartels in other source countries will merely pick up the customers." Gustavo Gorriti, a leading Peruvian expert on the drug trade, stated, "No judicial or law enforcement system in the world can suppress an activity in which whole societies and national economies are engaged."[253]

Certainly killing the cartel bosses won't change the basic forces of supply and demand. "Everyone is somewhat replaceable," noted William Baker, the FBI's assistant intelligence director, "and they do have the infrastructure so that new leaders can take over." Or, as one drug agent based in Mexico put it, "there are a lot of middle-level or lower-level Colombia's cashing in, looking for their place in the sun."[254]

Even if, by some miracle, U.S. efforts did succeed in wiping out the supply of foreign drugs at their source, nothing much would be accomplished in the long run. The domestic synthetic drug industry, already sizeable, would simply expand to meet the demand. Robert Stutman, former head of the New York DEA office, asserts that "within 60 days" of sealing the border "all of that cocaine I believe would be replaced by drugs made in the United States that have the exact same effect as cocaine, probably be more addicting, be longer lasting, and may in the long run actually be cheaper." The same holds for heroin. A single suitcase of synthetic fentanyl, a powerful substitute for heroin, could satisfy the entire U.S. market for a year. "We may see the day when synthetic heroin is as readily available as candy," warned California's attorney general, John Van de Kamp. Foreign drug enforcement is, in short, largely irrelevant to the U.S. drug problem.[255]

But it is highly relevant to countries whose societies have been torn apart by America's twin demands for drugs and drug enforcement. The former destabilizes poorly developed economies with vast numbers of narcodollars, enriching and empowering criminal syndicates. The latter destabilizes poorly developed societies by bankrolling powerful security forces with U.S. aid dollars, shifting the balance of power from civilian to more authoritarian military or paramilitary elites. In societies where the military traditionally pose the greatest threat to democracy and human rights, U.S. drug assistance can stunt or reverse the growth of political freedom itself.

The almost nine-fold jump in military aid to Bolivia between fiscal 1989 and fiscal 1990, for example, comes at a time when the Bolivia's coup-prone army

> is demanding a greater say, not only in the anti-drug campaign, but in politics generally... What has alarmed many about the military proposals, though, is the specifically military provision they wish to add to the constitution. This would define the armed forces as 'the fundamental institution of the state, charged with the mission of preserving Bolivia's national independence, sovereignty and honour, territorial integrity, peace, internal and external security; guaranteeing the stability of the legally constituted government; and co-operating in the integral development of the country.'[256]

No wonder Bolivian President Jaime Paz Zamora, commenting on Washington's push to ensure "the participation of the armed forces in the struggle against drug trafficking," stressed that "we must be very careful" to keep the armed forces within "a role assigned by the Constitution." Former Interior Undersecretary Jorge Alderrete warns that "The government has put at risk all the country's chances to achieve a peaceful solution to the drug trafficking problem. It will do nothing more than prove an old axiom: Violence begets violence."[257]

Thoughtful Colombians share similar concerns as they watch a torrent of aid go to their military, despite its record of corruption and human rights abuses. It is not only leaders of the left, like M-19's Antonio Navarro, who sense "a real danger" of a military putsch. Former President Alberto Lleras Restrepo issued the same warning in print. One informed foreign observer notes that "close links were forged in the mid-1970s between elements of the Colombian military and their peers in Argentina—and the former, particularly those who benefited from war college training in Buenos Aires, eagerly adopted the 'Third World War' rhetoric of their southern comrades." The military ruled Colombia in the past; it could take power again if popular dissatisfaction with continuing violence and civilian corruption turn public opinion in favor of drastic solutions.[258]

Ironically, even military leaders in Latin America and Asia sometimes question Washington's public anti-drug agenda. They note that aggressive enforcement could unintentionally spread dangerous insurgencies hostile to U.S. interests. Thus the Bolivian government has resisted American pressure to force widespread eradication of coca, arguing that such a campaign could foster "the emergence of a new and deadly guerrilla movement joining extremists, destitute peasants and drug traffickers."[259] Bolivia's ambassador to Washington, Carlos Delius, explained in 1989 that coca farmers

are extremely well organized in strong unions. Their leaders are indoctrinated in Marxist ideology and could become openly hostile to our democratic Government. As a result, sanctions are used as an excuse by anti-government trade unions to inflame and mobilize the farmers. Quite frankly, we are writing a prescription for disaster and potentially creating thousands of new recruits for terrorist organizations if we continue to pressure the growers...[260]

Such fears seem justified. Recent evidence suggests that Bolivian traffickers are not only waging a propaganda war to depict DEA agents as foreign oppressors, but actually financing and arming terrorist groups like the Zarate Willka Armed Forces of Liberation.[261]

The situation in Peru is much worse. Typical wall slogans in the Tingo Maria area, where guerrillas protect peasant cultivators from government police, read "Down with Imperialism! Down with Eradication!" As one U.S. congressional study observed, "eradication efforts have driven the coca growers into the arms of the Sendero Luminoso insurgents, who have adeptly exploited the fact that this U.S.-inspired program threatens the peasants' existence in a time of extreme economic hardship." The Peruvian political analyst Jose Gonzalez declared that "Nothing would make the guerrillas happier than to internationalize the conflict so that North American military advisers or, in an extreme case, American combat troops, get involved in the fight, enabling them to exploit this as an example of 'imperialistic intervention.'"[262]

These examples illustrate the potential for disaster inherent in America's anti-drug crusade. The policy of prohibition that Washington has exported so vigorously to the rest of the world guarantees that the drug trade will generate fabulous and quite artificial profits. Those profits in turn guarantee that organized crime, social upheaval and political corruption will bedevil countries that produce or transship drugs.

Though Washington's overwhelming political and economic power stifles most dissent, a few brave voices in the Third World have spoken out against the consequences of these programs. "Colombia cannot afford to go on obeying the orders of the United States to solve a U.S. drug problem at the cost of our institutions," said Fabio Echeverri, president of the National Association of Industrialists. "Our problem is different. The economy is at stake, and we have the obligation to seek solutions that serve our own interests."[262] Colombian opinion today is confused and mixed: repelled by the viciousness of the drug lords, attracted to the idea of negotiations and not closed to the idea of some form of drug legalization.

Legalization as an alternative has gained enormous ground in the United States as well. Prosecutors, judges, economists, statesmen and academics have come out of the closet to endorse alternatives to the "war on drugs." One reason is that U.S. society has begun to feel some of the same evils suffered in countries like Colombia and Peru: drug-related violence, ever-more-draconian abridgments of civil liberties, and a rapidly rising diversion of resources into police, courts and prisons to cope with the impossible demands on law enforcement.

The prospect for any wholesale reevaluation of the "war on drugs" isn't promising, at least in the short run. But most law enforcement officials today recognize, and indeed stress publicly, the absolute necessity of focusing on drug demand before any solution can be found. Yet demand-side programs receive less than half of federal anti-drug dollars.

Even so, few politicians dare question the wisdom of treating the drug problem as a war to be waged both at home and abroad. Even among some who admit the failures of supply-side drug control, the urge to expand failed government programs overwhelms good judgment and the test of experience. "To deal with this problem, we have to blanket the world," insisted Attorney General William French Smith. "We have no other choice."[263]

If Americans take their democratic values seriously, they do still have a choice. But they must not forfeit their right to choose by letting the rhetoric of drug wars lead them down the road of patriotic abdication.

MODERN OPIUM WARS

LANCING THE POPPY (*Opposite Page*) A young hillside farmer in Thailand holds an opium poppy that has just been lanced. The white liquid is raw opium. It will turn dark brown by nightfall. (*AP/Wide World*)

GULBUDDIN HEKMATYAR (*Right*) This rebel Afghan leader has financed his activities through U. S. aid and revenues gained by control of various Afghan opium routes. (*AP/Wide World*)

KHUN SA (*Below*) Widely considered the largest drug lord currently operating out of the Golden Triangle, Khun Sa gestures as he tells interviewers that American narcotics officials "say I have horns and fangs." (*AP/Wide World*)

ARCHITECTS & ALLIES

CHIANG KAI-SHEK (*Opposite Page*) Supplied with arms by the CIA, Chiang's nationalist party, the KMT, eventually came to control 80% of the heroin trade emanating out of the Golden Triangle (*AP/Wide World*)

JOSE LOPEZ-REGA (*Right*) Juan Peron's trusted minister, Lopez-Rega directed a right-wing death squad—the AAA—which likely benefited from U. S. aid for the war on drugs. (*AP/Wide World*)

LUCKY LUCIANO (*Below*) This gangland leader was restored to his throne as America's King of Heroin by U. S. Naval Intelligence in return for information he supplied the Navy at the end of the Second World War. (*AP/Wide World*)

CONTRA CONNECTIONS

Juan Ramon Matta Ballesteros (*Opposite Page*) A Class 1 DEA drug violator convicted in the abduction of DEA agent Enrique Camerena, Matta, a Honduran billionaire, was an important contributor to the U.S.-backed Nicaraguan Contras. (*AP/Wide World*)

Manuel Noriega (*Right*) Panama's former leader, and a known drug violator, Noriega worked with Lt. Col. Oliver North on supplying the Contras through airfields in Costa Rica. (*AP/Wide World*)

Oliver North (*Below*) This White House aide coördinated a vast, private army of support for the Contras, an army which included individuals with strong ties to the drug cartels. (*AP/ Wide World*)

ON THE HOME FRONT

GEORGE BUSH (*Above*) As United Nations Ambassador, member of Richard Nixon's pioneering Cabinet Committee on International Narcotics Control, CIA Director during the administration of Gerald Ford, and Ronald Reagan's point man in the war on drugs, President George Bush's intimate knowledge of the history and practice of U.S. drug policy spans the course of four different Republican administrations. In the picture, the President is holding up a bag of crack cocaine confiscated, for photo opportunity purposes, directly in front of the White House. (*AP/Wide World Photos*)

Endnotes

PREFACE

[1]The White House, *National Drug Control Strategy*, September 1989, 61-2; Senate Government Operations Committee, Permanent Subcommittee on Investigations (hereafter SPSI), hearings, *Federal Drug Interdiction: Role of the Department of Defense* (Washington: USGPO, 1989), 18.

CHAPTER ONE

[2]*U.S. News and World Report*, April 30, 1990.
[3]William Walker III, *Drug Control in the Americas* (Albuquerque: University of New Mexico Press, 1989), 122.
[4]James Mills, *Underground Empire* (Garden City: Doubleday, 1986), 555.
[5]*San Jose Mercury*, January 17, 1985.
[6]Jonathan Marshall, "Opium and the Politics of Gangsterism in Nationalist China," *Bulletin of Concerned Asian Scholars*, VIII (July-September 1976), pp. 19-48; *New York Times*, September 14, 1945.
[7]*Hoy* [La Paz], March 8, 1990 (citing sociologist Nelson Romero); *El Diario* [La Paz], November 27, 1989 (citing Bolivia's Chamber of Deputies International Affairs Commission); Richard Craig, "Illicit Drug Traffic," *Journal of Interamerican Studies*, Summer 1987.
[8]GAO, *Drug Control in Colombia and Bolivia*, NSIAD-89-24, November 1988; *Washington Post*, March 1, 1990.
[9]*New York Times*, August 31, 1981; *Le Monde*, October 2, 1980; *Los Angeles Times*, May 7, 1989; *New York Times*, February 14, 1979; Rensselaer Lee III, *The White Labyrinth* (New Brunswick: Transaction Publishers, 1989), 119; House Select Committee on Narcotics Abuse and Control (hereafter HSCNAC), report, *International Narcotics Control Study Missions to Latin America and Jamaica* (Washington: USGPO, 1984), p. 49.
[10]*Sunday Times* [London], August 10, 1980; *New York Times*, August 3, 1981; *St. Louis Post Dispatch*, May 27, 1984.
[11]House Committee on Foreign Affairs [hereafter HCFA], staff report, *US Narcotics Control Programs Overseas: An Assessment*, February 22, 1985, p. 17; *High Times*, May 1984, p. 19; *New York Times*, July 21, 1984; *San Francisco Examiner*, August 26, 1984.
[12]*San Francisco Examiner*, April 26, 1987; David Kline, "How to Lose the Coke War," *Atlantic Monthly*, May 1987; *Washington Post Weekly*, January 23-29, 1989.
[13]*Ibid.*; HCFA, staff report, *U.S. Narcotics Control Programs in Peru, Bolivia, Colombia, and Mexico: An Update*, February 1989, 15; HCFA, hearings, *Review of the Section 2013 Report and the State Department Mid-Year Update Report* (Washington: USGPO, 1989), 58; *Washington Post*, August 15, 1987; *Los Angeles Times*, March 11, 1987.
[14]*Los Tiempos* [Cochabamba], December 11, 1989.
[15]*Latin America Regional Reports* (hereafter LARR), RA-88-09, November 10, 1988.
[16]Antonil, *Mama Coca* (London: Hassle Free Press, 1978), pp. 79-81; *Latin America Political*

Report, (hereafter LAPR) May 5, 1978.
[17]Antonil, *Mama Coca*, p. 80-81; *NACLA Report*, May-June 1983, p. 20.
[18]*NACLA Report*, May-June 1983, p.20; Penny Lernoux, "Corrupting Colombia," p. 16; HSCNAC, report, *Oversight on Federal Drug Strategy—1979* (Washington, DC: USGPO, 1980), p. 5.
[19]*LAWR*, June 9, 1988, citing *Mensajes Colombianos*.
[20]*LAWR*, July 20, 1984.
[21]HCFA, hearing, *Recent Developments in Colombia* (Washington: USGPO, 1988), 9.
[22]*LARR*, Andean Group, June 23, 1988; *San Francisco Chronicle*, May 25, 1990; Bogota Inravision Television Cadena 1, June 4, 1989; Renssellaer Lee, "Why the US Cannot Stop South American Cocaine," *Orbis*, Fall 1988.
[23]*Miami Herald*, November 30, 1989.
[24]HSCNAC, report, *Study Mission to Central America and the Caribbean* (Washington: USGPO, 1989), 3; HSCNAC, *Narcotics Control in Mexico* (Washington: USGPO, 1988), 56; *Los Angeles Times*, June 9, 1990; *New York Times*, November 23, 1984.
[25]Alan Riding, *Distant Neighbors* (New York: Vintage Books, 1986), 165; James Mills, *Underground Empire*, 549; *Miami Herald*, March 24, 1985.
[26]*Chicago Tribune*, April 1, 1984; *LAWR*, February 3, 1984. A Florida grand jury actually named him as a member of an international heroin ring. See Peter Lupsha, "Drug Lords and Narco-Corruption: The Players Change but the Game Continues," paper presented at University of Wisconsin, May 11, 1990.
[27]*Oakland Tribune*, February 26, 1985. Cf. HCFA, *U.S. Narcotics Control Programs Overseas: An Assessment*, February 22, 1985.
[28]*New York Times*, March 16, 1985, April 21, 1985, April 30, 1985; *San Francisco Chronicle*, May 17, 1985; *Los Angeles Times*, March 19, 1985; *Washington Post*, February 17, 1980; *Time*, March 17, 1988; Elaine Shannon, *Desperados* (New York: Viking, 1988), *passim*. For the case of Sinaloa, see *New York Times*, April 16, 1989; *Excelsior* [Mexico City], March 10, 1989; SPSI, *Structure of International Drug Trafficking Organizations* (Washington: USGPO, 1989), 98.
[29]HSCNAC, hearing, *US Foreign Policy and International Narcotics Control—Part II* (Washington: USGPO, 1988), 30, 55; HCFA, *Narcotics Review in South America* (Washington: USGPO, 1988), 1.
[30]*San Francisco Examiner*, April 11, 1989; *Excelsior*, March 1, 1990; *Los Angeles Times*, July 7, 1989.
[31]HCFA, staff report, *U.S. Narcotics Control Programs in Peru, Bolivia, Colombia and Mexico: An Update* (Washington: USGPO, 1989), 31; *Por Esto* [Mexico City], May 10, 1989; Andrew Reding, "Mexico under Salinas: A Facade of Reform," *World Policy Journal*, Fall 1989; SPSI, *Structure of International Drug Trafficking Organizations*, 119.
[32]*Washington Post*, July 24, 1979.
[33]*Hoy* [La Paz], March 8, 1990.
[34]Antonil, *Mama Coca*, p. 96.
[35]*Wall Street Journal*, May 1, 1987; cf. HCFA, staff report, *U.S. Narcotics Control Programs Overseas: An Assessment*, 20.
[36]Richard Craig, "Illict Drug Traffic," *op. cit.*
[37]*SPSI, hearings, U.S. Government Anti-Narcotics Activities in the Andean Region of South America*, 289; *U.S. News and World Report*, April 30, 1990; *Miami Herald*, March 28, 1990.
[38]*Boston Globe*, January 24, 1982.
[39]*LAWR*, March 5, 1982.
[40]*Newsweek*, February 25, 1985; *Oakland Tribune*, June 2, 1985; *Los Angeles Times*, December 1,

1985.
[41]Ann Wrobleski, Assistant Secretary of State for International Narcotics Matters, testimony, HCFA, hearing, *Narcotics Review in South America* (Washington: USGPO, 1988), 100.
[42]HCFA, staff report, *U.S. Narcotics Control Programs in Peru, Bolivia, Colombia and Mexico: An Update*, 7-12.
[43]*LAWR*, November 3, 1988.
[44]*LAWR*, December 1, 1988.
[45]James Petras, "Drug-War Rhetoric Conceals Cartels' Capital Ties," *In These Times*, November 15, 1989.
[46]Eleanore Hill staff report in SPSI, hearings, *International Narcotics Trafficking* (Washington, DC: USGPO, 1981), p. 441. A DEA source in Bangkok claimed that "black" money accounts for "half of all Thai currency transfers." See Mills, *Underground Empire*, 1137.
[47]HSCNAC, report, *Study Mission on International Controls of Narcotics Trafficking and Production, January 2-22, 1978* (Washington, DC: USGPO, 1978), pp. 36-7.
[48]*Washington Post*, April 12, 1976.
[49]James Mills, *Underground Empire*, 777.
[50]HSCNAC, report, *Opium Production, Narcotics Financing and Trafficking in Southeast Asia* (Washington, DC: USGPO, 1977), p. 39.
[51]Mills, *Underground Empire*, 268, 274 [Gen. Prakorp]; *Insight*, February 5, 1990 [Maj. Gen. Veth Petbarom]; *Washington Post*, April 12, 1976 [Thanom Kittikachorn].
[52]*Nation*, February 2, 1989.
[53]David Westrate testimony, HCFA, hearing, *The Worldwide Drug Situation and International Narcotics Control Programs* (Washington: USGPO, 1987), 41; GAO, *Drug Control in Burma, Pakistan and Thailand*, NSIAS-88-94, February 1988, 30, 50. DEA itself admitted in 1987 that "Good relationships with Thai police and military officials are essential" to the Burma-based Shan United Army's "narcotics smuggling as well as resupply operations. Without police protection and cooperation, the SUA would have great difficulty obtaining weapons and provisions from Thailand." This is no small point since the SUA moves more than a third of all the opium produced in Burma (HCFA, *U.S. Narcotics Control Efforts in Southeast Asia* (Washington: USGPO, 1987), 127, 248-249). For other evidence of corruption, see *Bangkok Post*, March 23, 1990; *Matichon* [Bangkok], November 28, 1986; *Economist*, March 9, 1985.

CHAPTER TWO
[54]AP, April 24, 1990.
[55]*Newsweek*, December 16, 1985.
[56]*Washington Post*, March 1, 1990.
[57]*New York Times*, September 10, 1984; for more on Jamaican corruption, see HCFA, *Narcotics Control Programs Overseas: An Assessment*, 28.
[58]*Washington Post*, October 19, 1989.
[59]HCFA, hearings, *Narcotics Review in South America* (Washington: USGPO, 1988), 45.
[60]Lee, *The White Labyrinth*, 156-157; cf. comments of David Westrate, DEA Assistant Administrator for Operations, in Congressional Research Service, *Combatting International Drug Cartels: Issues for U.S. Policy* (Washington: USGPO, 1987), 2.
[61]Col. John D. Waghelstein, commander, 7th Special Forces Group (Airborne), 1st Special Forces, Fort Bragg, in *Military Review*, February 1987, 46-47.
[62]A. J. Langguth, *Hidden Terrors* (New York: Pantheon, 1978), pp. 48ff.

[63]*Brazilian Information Bulletin*, no. 1, p. 9.

[64]Testimony of Byron Engle, OPS director, in House Committee on Appropriations, Subcommittee on Foreign Operations and Related Agencies, hearings, *Foreign Assistance and Related Agencies, Appropriations for 1973* (Washington, DC: USGPO, 1974), p. 791; Michael Klare and Cynthia Arnson, *Supplying Repression* (Washington, D.C.: Institute for Policy Studies, 1981), p. 23; Congressional Research Service, *U.S. Assistance for Foreign Police Forces* (Washington: Library of Congress, 1989), 4, 6.

[65]Engle testimony, op. cit., pp. 792-5, 814-817.

[66]Congressional Research Service, *U.S. Assistance for Foreign Police Forces*, 5-7.

[67]Senate report 94-39, 94th Congress, 1st Session (Washington, DC: USGPO, 1975), p. 88.

[68]GAO, *Stopping U.S. Assistance to Foreign Police and Prisons*, February 19, 1976, 22-23.

[69]Klare and Arnson, *Supplying Repression*, 29.

[70]Argentine Commission for Human Rights, Washington DC Information Bureau, memorandum, ``US Narcotics Enforcement Assistance to Latin America," March 10, 1977; Klare and Arnson, *Supplying Repression*, pp. 33-37.

[71]Statement of Joseph Linnemann in SPSI, hearings, *International Narcotics Trafficking*, p. 559.

[72]Statement of DEA Administrator Peter Bensinger before HSCNAC, July 13, 1977, DEA print.

[73]*New York Times*, July 2, 1984

[74]Argentine Commission for Human Rights, ``US Narcotics Enforcement Assistance to Latin America"; *Sevendays*, April 19, 1976, p. 16.

[75]*LAPR*, May 18, 1979.

[76]*Latin America*, December 19, 1975. These drug allegations remain controversial, however. Former DEA undercover agent Michael Levine, based in Argentina in the late 1970s, found no solid evidence to link Lopez Rega to drugs (interview with Levine, March 1990).

[77]Antonil, *Mama Coca*, p. 106.

[78]*Washington Post*, June 20, 1979.

[79]Penny Lernoux, "Corrupting Colombia," p. 16; *NACLA Report*, May-June 1983, p. 20.

[80]New York Times, November 26, 1978; Penny Lernoux, ``Corrupting Colombia," p. 18.

[81]HSCNAC, hearings, *Oversight Hearings on Federal Drug Strategy—1979*, 404.

[82]Narcotics enforcement fell to the paramilitary National Police (F-2), with $13 million in U.S. funds and equipment. *New York Times*, September 11, 1984; HSCNAC, report, *International Narcotics Control Study Missions to Latin America and Jamaica* (Washington, D.C.: USGPO, 1984), p. 72; *San Francisco Chronicle*, March 21, 1984.

[83]*New York Times*, May 22, 1984; cf. *New York Times*, March 21, 1984; *Seattle Times*, March 26, 1984.

[84]Some critics accused Ambassador Lewis Tambs of grinding an ideological ax; a close political ally of Sen. Jesse Helms, R-N.C., he once called for an invasion or blockade of Cuba and Nicaragua to rid the Caribbean of the "Cuban-Sandinista cancer." See *NACLA Report*, May-June 1983, pp. 31-32.

[85]GAO, *Drug Control in Colombia and Bolivia*; *LAWR*, April 27, 1989; *Semana*, February 14, 1989; Lee, *TheWhite Labyrinth*, 118, 171-174. On the ELN and FARC, see *New York Times*, May 14, 1984; *El Tiempo* [Bogota], February 19, 1990; HCFA, staff report, *U.S. Narcotics Control Programs in Peru, Bolivia, Colombia and Mexico: An Update*, 23-24.

[86]See Lee, *The White Labyrinth*, 161-162, 172, on the vendetta between FARC and Rodriguez Gacha.

[87]Senate Foreign Relations Committee, Subcommittee on Terrorism, Narcotics and

International Communications, hearings, *Drugs, Law Enforcement and Foreign Policy* (Washington: USGPO, 1988), IV, 197. Hereafter "Kerry hearings" or "Kerry report." Cf. Merrill Collett, "The Myth of the Narco-Guerrillas," *Nation*, August 13, 1988. On CIA reports dismissing the narcoterrorist hypothesis, see Elaine Shannon, *Desperados*, 144-146.

[88]Penny Lernoux, "The Minister Who Had to Die," *Nation*, June 16, 1984, pp. 734-5; *NACLA Report*, May-June 1983, pp. 22-23.

[89]LAWR, November 24, 1988; HCFA, staff report, *U.S. Narcotics Control Programs...*, 23-24; America's Watch, *The Killings in Colombia* (New York, 1989), 4-5; *Wall Street Journal*, May 18, 1990.

[90]*LARR*, Andean Group, March 2, 1989; Bogota Inravision TV, Cadena 1, February 28, 1990 and March 1, 1990.

[91]Washington Office on Latin America, *WOLA Brief*, November 1989.

[92]See, for example, Bruce Bagley, "Dateline Drug Wars: Colombia: The Wrong Strategy," *Foreign Policy*, Winter 1989-90, 160; *El Tiempo*, January 22, 1990; *Philadelphia Inquirer*, November 24, 1989; *Miami Herald*, November 30, 1989; cf. *Washington Post*, November 13, 1989; Reuters, September 20, 1989. Cf.GAO, *Drug Control in Colombia and Bolivia*, 24.

[93]Cf. Bruce Bagley testimony, SPSI, hearings, *US Government Anti-Narcotics Activities...*, 133.

[94]HCFA, *Recent Developments in Colombia*, 58.

[95]HCFA, hearings, *Review of the Section 2013 Report...*, 55.

[96]Coletta Youngers, "Colombia's Deadly Politics," *Oakland Tribune*, April 6, 1990; "Bombardeos y secuestros masivos," *Solidaridad*, February 1990, 17-19; *Andean Newsletter*, #40, 3.

[97]US Department of State, "International Narcotics Control Strategy," November 13, 1981, Current Policy series, no. 345.

[98]Klare and Arnson, *Supplying Repression*, p. 38.; *Newsweek*, April 10, 1978.

[99]M. J. McConahay, "Mexico's War on Poppies—and Peasants," *New Times*, September 3, 1976, pp. 33-38.

[100]*NACLA Report*, March-April 1978, p. 41. Regarding recent repression against peasant organizations by army and state police, including extrajudicial executions, torture and "disappearances," see Amnesty International Report, 1984, 174-177 and AI memorandum, "Unacknowledged detention/Health concern, 10 August 1984, AI Index AMR 41/22/84. Gustavo Zarate, an Amnesty Prisoner of Conscience, was a 29-year old professor of social studies at the Autonomous University of Chiapas who was arrested 24 July 83 "based on planted police evidence" of marijuana and explosives. See AI memo, "Hunger strike," 31 August 1984, AI Index AMR 41/24/84 and Amnesty International Report, 1984, 176.

[101]Craig Pyes, "Legal Murders," *Village Voice*, June 4, 1979, pp. 1, 11-15.

[102]*Latin America Political Report*, March 17, 1978 and May 5, 1989.

[103]*San Jose Mercury*, December 17, 1989.

[104]*Los Angeles Times*, June 7, 1990; *San Francisco Chronicle*, July 4, 1990.

[105]Americas Watch, *Human Rights in Mexico: A Policy of Impunity* (June 1990), 3-4; for examples, see 19-32. See also *Time*, June 4, 1990; Amnesty International, "Hunger Strike," August 31, 1984 (AI Index AMR 41/24/84); Amnesty International, *Report, 1984*, 176.

[106]*San Francisco Chronicle*, July 7, 1990.

[107]*LAWR*, August 17, 1984; *New York Times*, September 13, 1984; *LAWR*, June 22, 1984.

[108]*New York Times*, August 13, 1984.

[109]Testimony of Gustavo Gorriti, SPSI, hearings, *U.S. Government Anti-Narcotics Activities in the Andean Region of South America*, 226; *Wall Street Journal*, August 10, 1984; testimony of Hon. Edwin G. Corr, former ambassador to Peru, in SPSI hearings, *International Narcotics*

Trafficking, p. 199; statement of Clyde Taylor, Acting Assistant Secretary of State for INM, Senate Committee on Labor and Human Resources, Subcommittee on Alcoholism and Drug Abuse, hearing, *Drugs and Terrorism, 1984* (Washington: USGPO 1984), 25; cf. 46-49. Congressional investigators cited "disturbing—though unconfirmed—reports that the military has actually collaborated with drug traffickers to identify guerrilla strongholds." (HCFA, staff report, *US Narcotics Control Programs Overseas: An Assessment*, February 22, 1985, p. 20. On bloody clashes between Sendero and the narcos, see Agence France Presse, May 13, 1987.

[110]*San Francisco Examiner*, July 7, 1984; *Norfolk Virginian-Pilot*, July 29, 1984.

[111]*Washington Post*, December 29, 1984; Rensselaer Lee II, "Why the U.S. Cannot Stop South American Cocaine."

[112]*New York Times*, April 12, 1990; SPSI, hearings, *U.S. Government Anti-Narcotics Activities in the Andean Region of South America*, 50.

[113]*New York Times*, April 22, 1990; SPSI, hearings, *U.S. Government Anti-Narcotics Activities in the Andean Region of South America*, 155.

[114]*Ibid.*, 170.

[115]*Ibid.*, 294; *Los Angeles Times*, January 6, 1990; *New York Times*, December 6, 1989.

[116]*Christian Science Monitor*, May 3, 1990; *New York Times*, May 7, 1990; *San Francisco Chronicle*, August 15, 1990. See also Amnesty International, Peru Briefing, "Caught between two fires," November 1989.

[117]*San Francisco Chronicle*, March 21, 1984.

[118]*Far Eastern Economic Review*, September 14, 1979, p. 39; *Washington Post*, April 11, 1976; Delaney, "Capturing an Opium King," p. 68.

[119]HSCNAC, report, *International Narcotics Control Study Missions to Latin America and Jamaica*, 143.

[120]William Delaney, "Capturing an Opium King," p. 66; *Far Eastern Economic Review*, June 18, 1982; Interview with Walter Mackem, former CIA drug analyst, December 19, 1978.

[121]Klare and Arnson, *Supplying Repression*, p. 39; *New York Times*, August 4, 1975; Eleanore Hill report, in SPSI, hearings, *International Narcotics Trafficking*, p. 425; GAO, *Drug Control: Enforcement Efforts in Burma Are Not Effective*, NSIAS-89-197, September 1989, 17.

[122]HSCNAC, hearings, *Southeast Asian Narcotics* (Washington, DC: USGPO, 1978), pp. 45-46.

[123]HSCNAC, report, *Opium Production, Narcotics Financing and Trafficking in Southeast Asia* (Washington, DC: USGPO, 1977), p. 37.

[124]HCFA, *U.S. Narcotics Control Efforts in Southeast Asia*, 226; Edith Mirante, "Eradicating the Tribes: Burma's Use of US donated herbicide," 1988; *New York Times*, August 28, 1987.

[125]House International Relations Committee, Subcommittee on Future Foreign Police Research and Development, hearings, *Proposal to Control Opium From the Golden Triangle and Terminate the Shan Opium Trade* (Washington, DC: USGPO, 1975); HSCNAC, hearings, *Cocaine and Marijuana Trafficking in Southeastern United States* (Washington, DC: USGPO, 1978); cf. analysis by Robert Schwab in HSCNAC, hearings, *Southeast Asian Narcotics*, pp. 185-221; Senate Committee on the Judiciary, Subcommittee on Internal Security, hearings, *World Drug Traffic and Its Impact on U.S. Security*, part 1 (Washington, DC: USGPO, 1972), pp. 33ff; *Washington Post*, July 31, 1972.

[126]Mathea Falco, coordinator for INM, July 13, 1977 (State Department release).

[127]GAO, *Drug Control in Burma, Pakistan and Thailand*, February 1988; *New York Times*, March 14, 1988; *Bangkok Post*, March 23, 1990 and May 5, 1990; *The Nation* [Bangkok], February 2, 1990; *Insight*, February 5, 1990; Edith Mirante, "Eradicating the Tribes: Burma's Use of U.S. Donated Herbicide," 1988.

[128]Edith Mirante, "The Shan Frontier: Exploitation and Eradication," February 1989; *Congressional Record*, August 11, 1988.

[129]*San Francisco Chronicle*, May 15, 1990; Assistant Secretary Melvyn Levitsky, quoted in *Los Angeles Times*, March 27, 1990; *New York Times*, February 11, 1990, citing estimates of opium production rising from 1,600 tons to 2,200-2,600 tons; *New York Times*, April 1, 1990.

CHAPTER THREE

[130]Robert Singer, "The Rise of the Dope Dictators," *High Times*, March 1977, p. 57.

[131]Robert Singer, "The Rise of the Dope Dictators," p. 58.

[132]Harry Anslinger, *The Murderers* (New York: Farrar, Straus and Cudahy, 1962), pp. 294-5. For more on Anslinger's use of the Communist dope scare to advance his bureau's interests, see Douglas Clark Kinder, "Bureaucratic Cold Warrior: Harry J. Anslinger and Illicit Narcotics Traffic," *Pacific Historical Review* 169 (1981), 169-191; Douglas Clark Kinder and William O. Walker III, "Stable Force in a Storm: Harry J. Anslinger and United States Narcotic Foreign Policy, 1930-1962," *The Journal of American History* 72 (March 1986), 908-927.

[133]Anslinger, *The Murderers*, p. 228; Richard Deverall, *Red China's Dirty Drug War* (Tokyo, 1954); Sal Vizzini, *Vizzini* (New York: Pinnacle Books, 1972), 228. Deverall worked for the AFL's Free Trade Union Committee.

[134]*New York Times*, January 15, 1959; Harry Anslinger, "The Red Chinese Dope Traffic," *Military Police Journal*, February-March 1961; Peter Dale Scott foreward to Henrik Kruger, *The Great Heroin Coup* (Boston: South End Press, 1980), p. 15.

[135]*New York Times*, January 18, 1973, quoting Nelson Gross, the State Department's special adviser on narcotics; cf. *Los Angeles Times*, January 18, 1973.

[136]BNDD Fact Sheet 2, "Illegal Traffic in Narcotics and Dangerous Drugs," (Washington, DC: USGPO, 1970), p. 6; October 27, 1971 statement of Louis J. Link, chief of the Public Inquiries Division of the Department of State, cited in *Congressional Record*, March 29, 1972, p. 10880. Jack Anderson in *Washington Post*, May 26, 1972. For a balanced assessment, see Andrew Tully, *The Secret War Against Dope* (New York: Coward, McCann & Geoghegan, 1973), p. 247. George Belk, former assistant administrator of DEA, confirmed that "we never really had any firm intelligence that the Red Chinese were ever involved in or sanctioned drug trafficking." Interview with Belk, February 18, 1986.

[137]Conservatives also accused Salvador Allende's Chilean socialist government of earning foreign exchange through the cocaine traffic. See *Congressional Record*, July 15, 1974, p. 23285; *Washington Post*, January 19, 1975; *New York Times*, September 15, 1984; *New York Post*, September 15, 1984.

[138]*Washington Star-News*, August 16, 1972; testimony of Nathan Adams before Senate Committee on Labor and Human Resources, Subcommittee on Alcoholism and Drug Abuse, hearing, *Drugs and Terrorism* (Washington: USGPO, 1984), 107-109; *Forbes*, April 17, 1989 [Bulgaria]; HCFA, hearing, *U.S. Narcotics Control Efforts in Southeast Asia*, 84, 114; *Rangoon Post*, November 27, 1988; *Washington Post*, August 30, 1988 [Laos]; *San Francisco Examiner*, March 23, 1986 [Tamils]; *U.S. News and World Report*, May 4, 1987; *Vancouver Sun*, January 19, 1988 [Sikhs].

[139]Joel Millman, "False Connection," *Nation*, September 22, 1984, p. 228-9.

[140]Jonathan Marshall, "Drugs and U.S. Foreign Policy," in Ronald Hamowy, ed., *Dealing With Drugs* (San Francisco: Pacific Research Institute for Public Policy, 1987), 162 [Somoza]; April 19, 1985 transcript of hearing before Senate Subcommittee on Alcohol and Drug Abuse.

[141]*Ibid.*; *Los Angeles Times*, March 23, 1989; John Dinges, *Our Man in Panama* (New York: Random House, 1990), 184.

[142]Kerry Report, 67-68; *Miami Herald*, July 29, 1988.

[143]*New York Times*, July 28, 1984; *Los Angeles Times*, July 28, 1984; HSCNAC, hearing, *US Foreign Policy and International Narcotics Control—Part II*, 115.

[144]Interview with Frank Sturgis, *High Times*, April 1977, p. 26.

[145]*Granma Weekly Review*, May 2, 1976.

[146]Interview with a former assistant US attorney, February 11, 1986; with former Dade County Metro police Lt. Raul Diaz, February 12, 1986; and with former Alcohol, Tobacco and Firearms agent Ed Seibert, February 27, 1986. The first two believe that Fidel Castro uses the profits to finance an intelligence network parallel to and independent of the KGB-dominated Cuban DGI. See also Ernest Volkman, "The Odd Couple," *Family Weekly*, April 29, 1984; Senate, Committee on the Judiciary, Subcommittee on Security and Terrorism; Committee on Foreign Relations, Subcommittee on Western Hemisphere Affairs; and US Senate Drug Enforcement Caucus, hearings, *The Cuban Government's Involvement in Facilitating International Drug Traffic* (Washington, DC: USGPO, 1983).

[147]*San Jose Mercury*, November 6, 1982; statement of Clyde Taylor, Acting Assistant Secretary of State for International Narcotics Matters, Senate Committee on Labor and Human Resources, Subcommittee on Alcoholism and Drug Abuse, hearing, *Drugs and Terrorism, 1984* (Washington: USGPO 1984), 25. See also Francis Mullen's statement in *Miami Herald*, April 24, 1982, May 1, 1982; and FBI Director William Webster in *Los Angeles Times*, February 14, 1986.

[148]*Washington Post*, June 28, 1989.

[149]*San Jose Mercury*, May 4, 1984; *New York Times*, May 10, 1984. For general treatments of the evidence against the Cuban government, see HCFA, hearings, *Cuban Involvement in International Narcotics Trafficking* (Washington: USGPO, 1989) and *Wall Street Journal*, April 30, 1984.

[150]Statement of Francis Mullen, DEA administrator, Senate Committee on Labor and Human Resources, Subcommittee on Alcoholism and Drug Abuse, hearing, *Drugs and Terrorism, 1984*, 13.

CHAPTER FOUR

[151]Catherine Lamour and Michel Lamberti, *The International Connection* (London: Penguin, 1974), 136.

[152]Kerry hearings, IV, 241.

[153]Congressional Research Service, *Combatting International Drug Cartels: Issues for U.S. Policy* (Washington: USGPO, 1987), 19.

[154]Interview on MacNeil/Lehrer Newshour, April 23, 1990.

[155]*New York Times*, March 25, 1990; *San Francisco Chronicle*, March 15, 1989; CIA Director William Webster speech to Association of Foreign Intelligence Officers, April 10, 1989, in *Signal*, September 1989; *Washington Times*, May 2, 1989.

[156]Ibid.

[157]Interview with Brennan, July 24, 1976; Ralph Blumenthal, *Last Days of the Sicilians* (New York: Times Books, 1988), 53; Richard Deacon, *A History of the British Secret Service* (New York: Taplinger, 1969), 370-1; Rodney Campbell, *The Luciano Project* (New York: McGraw Hill, 1977), 181-182.

[158]Campbell, *The Luciano Project*; Alan Block, "A Marriage of Convenience: A Collaboration Between Organized Crime and U.S. Intelligence," in Robert Kelley, ed., *Organized Crime: A*

Global Perspective (Totowa, N.J.: Rowman & Littlefield, 1986).

[159]Alfred McCoy, *The Politics of Heroin in Southeast Asia* (New York: Harper & Row, 1972), 24-28.

[160]Peter Dale Scott foreward to Henrik Kruger, *The Great Heroin Coup*, p. 14; Miles Copeland, *Beyond Cloak and Dagger* (New York: Pinnacle Books, 1975), pp. 240-241.

[161]McCoy, *The Politics of Heroin in Southeast Asia*, ch. 1 and 2.

[162]On the alliance of OSS and Navy's SACO with Chinese gangster Tu Yueh-sheng and Chinese secret service leader Tai Li, see Jonathan Marshall, "Opium and the Politics of Gangsterism in Nationalist China, 1927-1945," *Bulletin of Concerned Asian Scholars* 8 (July-September 1976), 18-38.

[163]Catherine Lamour and Michel Lamberti, *The International Connection*, 100. For general background on the CIA and Southeast Asia, see McCoy, op. cit.

[164]*San Francisco Chronicle*, June 13, 1966.

[165]*Christian Science Monitor*, May 29, 1970; John Tunney, quoted in *New Yorker*, April 11, 1970.

[166]Alfred McCoy, "A Correspondence with the CIA," *New York Review of Books*, September 21, 1972, 26-34; "Commentary," *Harper's*, October 1972, 116-121.

[167]Senate Select Committee to Study Governmental Operations with Respect to Intelligence Activities, final report, book I, *Foreign and Military Intelligence* (Washington: USGPO, 1976), 228-233.

[168]Elaine Shannon, *Desperados*, 466.

[169]HCFA, hearing, *U.S. Narcotics Control Efforts in Southeast Asia*, 61 [Lu and KMT]; Mills, *Underground Empire*, 222 [Lu and CIA, quoting from a memo by the chief of DEA's international intelligence division].

[170]House Government Operations Committee, hearings, *Justice Department Treatment of Criminal Cases Involving CIA Personnel and Claims of National Security* (Washington: USGPO, 1975), 136, 151-4, 221, 231, 232, 430; Percy quoted in Christopher Robbins, *Air America* (New York: G.P. Putnam's Sons, 1979), 244-5.

[171]*New York Times*, October 7, 8, and 21, 1976; *Newsweek*, October 31, 1977.

[172]Mills, *Underground Empire*, 33.

[173]Unsigned, undated DEA memorandum, probably by Lucien Conein in 1975, *CIA Narcotic Intelligence Collection*. Released by DEA under the Freedom of Information Act and supplied to the author by John Hill. For examples of some aborted prosecutions, see Jefferson Morely and Malcolm Byrne, "The Drug War and 'National Security,'" *Dissent*, Winter 1989; John Kelly interview with former DEA officer, September 29, 1988.

[174]*Drug Enforcement*, July 1978; *Der Spiegel*, May 9, 1977; Mills, *Underground Empire*, 360-1, 357, 521, 548, 73, 619.

[175]*New York Times*, April 21, 1985.

[176]*Time*, March 17, 1988; Elaine Shannon, *Desperados* (New York: Viking, 1988), 186-187.

[177]Shannon, *Desperados*, 294; Trial memorandum, United States of America v. Rafael Caro Quintero et. al., United States District Court for the Central District of California, CR 87-422(f)-ER.

[178]Terrence Poppa, *Druglord* (New York: Pharos Books, 1990), 145; Shannon, *Desperados*, 180-183; *Washington Post*, April 6, 1982; *New York Times*, April 1, 1985; DEA debriefing of Lawrence Harrison, September 26, 1989.

[179]*Excelsior* [Mexico City], August 1, 1989; SPSI, *Structure of International Drug Trafficking Organizations*, 120; Shannon, *Desperados*, 128-129, 186; *Washington Post*, July 18, 1990. Zorrilla has also been accused of the murder of muckraking Mexican journalist Manuel

Buendia (*Los Angeles Times*, June 13, 1989).

[180]*Los Angeles Times*, August 19, 1988, August 31, 1988, July 5, 1990 and July 8, 1990.

[181]Kerry Report, 2. A report issued a few months later by the Costa Rican Congress charged that 11,000 pounds of cocaine were shipped through that country in 1984 and 1985 by smuggling networks established with U.S. help to supply the Contras. See *Washington Times*, July 24, 1989.

[182]Kerry Report, 2, 36, 41.

[183]Quoted in Kerry Report, 38.

[184]Kerry Report, 42-43.

[185]Kerry Report, 44; *Los Angeles Herald Examiner*, August 30, 1989.

[186]*Los Angeles Times*, February 13, 1988.

[187]*San Jose Metro*, October 13, 1988.

[188]*Washington Post*, December 7, 1987; *Vanity Fair*, March 1990.

[189]Peter Dale Scott and Jonathan Marshall, *Cocaine Politics: Drugs, Armies, and the CIA in Central America* (Berkeley: University of California Press, forthcoming, 1991).

[190]Frederick Kempe, *Divorcing the Dictator* (New York: G. P. Putnam's Sons, 1990), 28-30; John Dinges, *Our Man in Panama*, 90.

[191]Kerry Report, 85, 94-96; Kempe, *Divorcing the Dictator*, 158-160; Dinges, *Our Man in Panama*, 252-3.

[192]Kerry Report, 79.

[193]Dinges, *Our Man in Panama*, 58-64.

[194]Mills, *Underground Empire*, 1132; Dinges, *Our Man in Panama*, 233, 253, 292; Kempe, *Divorcing the Dictator*, 170, 174; interviews with Thomas Cash (DEA) and Richard Gregorie, February 1989.

[195]*New York Times*, February 6, 1990; Kerry hearings, II, 215; House Foreign Affairs Committee, hearing, *Narcotics Review in Central America*, 93 [Endara]; *Oakland Tribune*, January 5 and 22, 1990; *Boston Globe*, February 5, 1990 [First Interamericas].

[196]Claire Sterling, *The Octopus* (New York: W. W. Norton, 1990); cf. Congressional Research Service, *Combatting International Drug Cartels: Issues for US Policy* (Washington: USGPO, 1987), 6.

[197]GAO, *Drug Control: US Supported Efforts in Burma, Pakistan and Thailand*, February 1988, 12; Ralph Blumenthal, *Last Days of the Sicilians*, 101; *Observer*, October 6, 1985; testimony of DEA official Charles Gutensoh, reprinted in Luciano Violante, *La Mafia dell'eroina* (Rome: Editori Riuniti, 1987), 198.

[198]*New York Times*, November 18, 1972.

[199]*Washington Post*, November 2, 1978 and January 2, 1981; WDNI [World Narcotics Intelligence report], October 24, 1980; WDNI, October 12, 1979; Reuters, July 3, 1979; *McLean's*, April 30, 1979, quoted in Konrad Ege, "U.S. Intervention in Afghanistan," *Counterspy*, v. 4, no. 1, 17. Two French drug experts had warned in the early 1970s that "To forbid opium growing in Afghan Pakhtunistan would be to play into the hands of the Pakistanis by arousing anti-Afghan sentiment among the Pathan tribes" (Catherine Lamour and Michel Lamberti, *The International Connection* (London: Penguin, 1974), 136).

[200]WDNI, October 24, 1980; SPSI, report, *Illegal Narcotics Profits* (Washington: USGPO, 1980), 14.

[201]*Philadelphia Magazine*, August 1980, 202.

[202]Joyce Lowinson and David Musto in *New York Times*, May 22, 1980.

[203]David Musto, statement at May 12, 1990 conference at University of Wisonsin.

[204]State Department, *International Narcotics Control Strategy Report*, v. I, 1986, 232-233.

[205]*San Francisco Chronicle*, December 16, 1983.

[206]HSCNAC, report, *International Narcotics Control Study Missions* (Washington: USGPO, 1984), 161).

[207]*Christian Science Monitor*, December 28, 1988; *Manchester Guardian Weekly*, October 29, 1989; *Saudi Gazette*, October 10, 1989; *Far Eastern Economic Review*, September 14, 1989; *Washington Times*, March 26, 1990; *Newsline* [Karachi], December 1989; *Washington Post*, May 13, 1990; Barnett Rubin, testimony before The Commission on Security and Cooperation in Europe, May 3, 1990. Pro-Soviet sources have long identified Gulbuddin as a heroin king. See *Haqiqat-e Enquelab-e Sawr* (Kabul), December 28, 1986; Havana Radio, October 24, 1989.

[208]*Washington Post*, May 13, 1990.

[209]*Nation*, November 14, 1988; *London Observer*, April 30, 1989;*Financial Times*, June 6, 1989; *Christian Science Monitor*, December 28, 1988; *Newsline* [Karachi], December 1989, 14.

[210]GAO, *Drug Control in Burma, Pakistan and Thailand*. February 1988, 27-29; HSCNAC, hearing, *Asian Heroin Production and Trafficking* (Washington: USGPO, 1990), 10.

[211]*Financial Times*, June 6, 1989; *Financial Times*, December 9, 1989.

[212]*Newsweek*, April 10, 1989; cf. March 13, 1989; *Newsday*, April 2, 1989; *La Repubblica*, November 8, 1988; *Le Monde*, November 18, 1988; *Swiss American Review*, January 25, 1989 (citing the Zurich weekly *SonntagsBlick*); *Europeo*, February 17, 1989.

[213]*New York Times*, March 26, 1989.

[214]AP, April 2, 1990.

[215]Statement May 12, 1990 at University of Wisonsin-Madison conference on drugs and national security.

[216]Claude D. Taylor, deputy assistant secretary of state for INM, quoted in *San Diego Union*, January 12, 1986.

[217]*LAWR*, March 23, 1984.

[218]*Wall Street Journal*, April 18, 1980; Peter Dale Scott, *The War Conspiracy* (Indianapolis: Bobbs-Merrill, 1972), p. 210; Edward Hymoff, *The OSS in World War II* (New York: Ballantine Books, 1972), 277; interview with Stanley Karnow, March 7, 1986.

[219]ID and Castle: U.S. Congress, House, Committee on Government Operations, hearings, *Oversight Hearings into the Operations of the IRS* (Washington, DC: USGPO, 1976), pp. 907-909. Lockheed: Yamakawa Akio, "Lockheed Scandal," *Ampo*, April-September 1976, p. 3; cf. Jim Hougan, *Spooks* (New York: William Morrow, 1978), p. 456.

[220]"Report on the Showa Trading Company" by Lt. Eric W. Fleisher, Investigative Division, U.S. Army, July 25, 1947, National Archives; Tad Szulc, "The Money Changer," *The New Republic*, April 10, 1976, pp. 10-11; Anthony Sampson, *The Arms Bazaar* (New York: Viking Press, 1977), pp. 218-221.

[221]Tad Szulc, "The Money Changer," pp. 10-11.

[222]*Ibid.*; *Washington Post*, June 9, 1976; McCoy, *The Politics of Heroin in Southeast Asia*, pp. 214-216; SPSI, hearings, *Illegal Currency Manipulations Affecting South Vietnam* (Washington, DC: USGPO, 1969), pp. 276-279; Interview with Stanley Karnow, March 7, 1986.

[223]*The Tribune* (Oakland), November 30, 1984.

[224]Jonathan Kwitny, *Crimes of Patriots* (New York: W. W. Norton, 1987), pp. 150-151, 164.

[225]A. J. Langguth, *Hidden Terrors* (New York: Pantheon, 1968), pp. 48-9, 57, 72, 124, 138, 242-3; Thomas Lobe, *United States National Security Policy and Aid to the Thailand Police* (University of Denver, 1977), p. 9; Commission on CIA Activities Within the United States, *Report to the President*, (New York: Manor Books, 1975), p. 235 (hereafter Rockefeller report).

[226]Frank C. Darling, cited in Noam Chomsky and Edward S. Herman, *The Washington Connection and Third World Fascism*, I (Boston: South End Press, 1979), pp. 221-2.

[227]McCoy, *The Politics of Heroin in Southeast Asia*, pp. 136-145.

[228]Thomas Lobe,*United States National Security Policy and Aid to the Thai Police*, pp. 30-31, 38, 41-2, 80; Jim Hougan, *Spooks*, pp. 142-3; John Burgess, "The Thailand Connection," *Counterspy*, Winter 1976, pp. 31-33.

[229]Thomas Lobe, op. cit., p. 117; cf. William Shawcross, "How Tyranny Returned to Thailand," *New York Review of Books*, December 9, 1976, pp. 59-62; interview with Norman Rossner, Bureau of International Narcotics Matters, Department of State, December 13, 1984; *San Francisco Chronicle*, October 21, 1976 and November 23, 1976;*Washington Post*, October 21, 1976; *New York Times*, November 1 and 10, 1976.

[230]DEA weekly intelligence digest, WDNI-79-14, April 13, 1979; Mills, *Underground Empire*, 780, 787, 1067; *New York Times*, August 10, 1987. On Special Forces counterinsurgency training of BPP, see Lobe, 41-2.

[231]*New York Times*, July 11, 1975; *Washington Post*, February 19, 1975; Rockefeller report, pp. 233-234.

[232]Alan Block and John McWilliams, "On the Origins of American Counterintelligence," *Journal of Policy History*, I (1989), 356-358.

[233]Harry Anslinger, *The Protectors* (New York: Farrar, Straus, 1964), pp. 24, 76, 107; Block and McWilliams, "On the Origins of American Counterintelligence," 360-362.

[234]Vizzini, *Vizzini* (New York: Pinnacle Books, 1972), 31-32, 166; interview with Charles Siragusa, February 1979; Alan Block, "Toward a History of American Drug Policy," paper delivered at University of Wisconsin, May 11, 1990; interview with Vizzini, December 20, 1978.

[235]*New York Times*, November 8, 1975; Block, "Toward a History of American Drug Policy."

[236]January 22, 1954 CIA document released under Freedom of Information Act on January 4, 1979.

[237]Senate Human Resources Committee, Subcommittee on Health and Scientific Research, hearings, *Human Drug Testing by the CIA* (Washington: USGPO, 1977), 176.; See White's diary entries for June 30, 1948, August 1, 1948, October 22, 1952, October 30, 1952, November 1, 1952; at Foothill College, Los Altos Hills, California.

[238]David Wise, "The CIA's Svengalis," *Inquiry*, September 18, 1978; *San Francisco Examiner*, September 18, 1977.

[239]Dan Moldea, *The Hoffa Wars* (New York: Paddington Press, 1978), p. 127; *Washington Post*, January 4, 1978. The CIA officer was almost certainly Col. Sheffield Edwards of the Office of Security. Interview with a former House and Senate staff investigator, March 7, 1986.

[240]"Project ZR/RIFLE," CIA document released to the Center for National Security Studies under the Freedom of Information Act; cf. U.S. Congress, Senate, Select Committee to Study Governmental Operations With Respect to Intelligence Activities, report, *Alleged Assassination Plots Involving Foreign Leaders*, pp. 43-48, 181-190.

[241]Taylor Branch, "Raising a Glass to *Beau Geste*," *Esquire*, August 1976, pp. 30-34; interview with Stanley Karnow, March 7, 1986; interview with a former House and Senate staff investigator, March 7, 1986. On Conein-Helliwell connection see E. Howard Hunt, *Undercover* (London: W.H. Allen, 1975), p. 42. On Conein and Montagnards, Interview with former Senate Permanent Investigations Subcommittee staffer William Gallinaro, February 19, 1986.

[242]Interview with former BNDD director John Ingersoll, February 12, 1986.

[243]*Washington Post*, June 13, 1976.

[244]"*Project BUNCIN—Operational Plan*" November 29, 1972; *Project Buncin: Summary, September 1972-March 1973.* Date: March 12, 1973; Lucien Conein memorandum, May 25, 1976 re Government Operations Subcommittee Hearings; *Overall Assessment of Project DEACON I*, December 2, 1974. These and other documents on BUNCIN/DEACON were released by the DEA under the Freedom of Information Act and generously supplied to the author by John Hill.

[245]Conein: *Washington Post*, January 23, 1975; Report of June 18, 1975 to the Attorney General, Subject: Additional Integrity Matters, submitted by Michael A. Defeo, et. al., pp. 8-9. WerBell: *Miami Herald*, September 4, 1976; interview with Edwin Marger, February 20, 1986.

[246]Edward J. Epstein, *Agency of Fear* (New York: G. P. Putnam's Sons, 1977), pp. 143-146.

[247]Jonathan Marshall, "The White House Death Squad," *Inquiry*, March 5, 1979, pp. 15-21; Kempe, *Divorcing the Dictator*, 80-81; Seymour Hersh, "Our Man in Panama," *Life*, March 1990, 81-93.

[248]SPSI, *Structure of International Drug Trafficking Organizations*, 14.

[249]*Boston Globe*, April 3, 1990; *Inside the Army*, March 29, 1990. One private contractor for Pentagon special operations, Peregrine International Associates, allegedly undertook "hits" against drug traffickers in Peru, Honduras, Belize and the Caribbean in the mid-1980s. See *San Jose Mercury*, April 26, 1987.

CHAPTER FIVE

[250] Interview with MacNeil/Lehrer Newshour, April 23, 1990.

[251]*Los Angeles Times*, March 2, 1990; *Washington Post*, February 15, 1990 and May 13, 1990.

[252]Paul Eddy, *Cocaine Wars* (New York: W. W. Norton, 1988), 98; SPSI, hearings, *Federal Drug Interdiction: Role of the Department of Defense* (Washington: USGPO, 1989), 83; *New York Times*, June 14, 1990.

[253]*New York Times*, September 16, 1984; Peter Reuter, G. Crawford, J. Dave, *Sealing the Border: The Effects of Military Participation in Drug Interdiction* (Santa Monica: RAND Corporation, 1988); HSCNAC, report, *Drugs and Latin America: Economic and Political Impact and U.S. Policy Options* (Washington: USGPO, 1989), 23; Shannon, *Desperados*, 401; SPSI, hearings, *U.S. Government Anti-Narcotics Activities in the Andean Region of South America*, 129.

[254]SPSI, *Structure of International Drug Trafficking Organizations*, 53-54; *San Diego Union*, October 21, 1989; For additional views on the replaceability of drug kingpins, see Rensselaer Lee comments in HSCNAC, report, *Drugs and Latin America: Economic and Political Impact and U.S. Policy Options* (Washington: USGPO, 1989), 127; Donald Mabry comments in House Armed Services Committee, Investigations Subcommittee, report, *The Andean Drug Strategy and the Role of the U.S. Military* (Washington: USGPO, 1990), 40.

[255]MacNeil/Lehrer Newshour, March 27, 1990 [Stutman]; *San Francisco Chronicle*, August 31, 1986; *Oakland Tribune*, March 13, 1986; cf. remarks of David Westrate, DEA Assistant Administrator for Operations, in Congressional Research Service, *Combatting International Drug Cartels: Issues for U.S. Policy*, 35; and Lt. Gen. Stephen Olmstead, Deputy Assistant Secretary of Defense for Drug Policy and Enforcement, in House Armed Services Committee, Investigations Subcommittee, report, *Narcotics Interdiction and the Use of the Military* (Washington: USGPO, 1988), 25.

[256]*LAWR*, October 13, 1988.

[257]EFE, May 6, 1990; AP, June 11, 1990.

[258]*La Vanguardia* [Barcelona], April 30, 1990; *Latin America Weekly Report*, May 24, 1990.

[259]*LARR*, Andean Group, September 4, 1986.

[260]SPSI, hearings, *U.S. Government Anti-Narcotics Activities in the Andean Region of South America*, 77.

[261]*Washington Post*, January 16, 1989; *Presencia* [La Paz], August 12, 1989. Cf. Ann Wrobleski testimony, HCFA, hearings, *Review of the 1989 International Narcotics Control Strategy Report* (Washington: USGPO, 1989), 103.

[262]*Los Angeles Times*, March 5, 1989; SPSI, report, *United States Government Anti-Narcotics Activities in the Andean Region of South America*, 7, 111.

[263]Penny Lernoux, "Corrupting Colombia," p. 19.

[264]*New York Times*, September 16, 1984.

Index